Real Chees
Facts Ab
U.S. Presidents

CRANE HILL
PUBLISHERS

Real Cheesy Facts About: U.S. Presidents

Copyright © 2006 by Crane Hill Publishers

ISBN-13: 978-1-57587-248-3
ISBN-10: 1-57587-248-X

Book design by Miles G. Parsons
Illustrations by Neal Cross and Miles G. Parsons

Printed in the United States of America

Library of Congress Cataloging-in-Publication Data

Platt, Camille Smith.
    Real cheesy facts about-- U.S. presidents / by Camille Smith Platt.
        p. cm.
    ISBN-13: 978-1-57587-248-3
    1. Presidents--United States--Miscellanea. 2. Presidents--United
    States--Biography--Anecdotes.   I. Title.
    E176.1 .P745
    973.09'9--dc22

2006024899

Real Cheesy Facts About: U.S. Presidents

Camille Smith Platt

CRANE HILL
PUBLISHERS

Table of Contents

Chapter 1

Young and Restless: Presidents Before They Were Stars

Young and Restless: Presidents Before They Were Stars

Not yet in the political limelight, the presidents filled their younger days with penny-pushing, romance, liquor, and a bit of mischief. From arguing with Mom over the family budget to nearly marrying the daughter of a famous Ku Klux Klan leader, these boys had a lot to learn before taking their pre-politician baggage to the White House.

DID YOU KNOW ?

As a teenager, Reagan worked as a lifeguard for seven summers and made seven rescues.

★ ★ ★ ★ ★

WHAT'S IN A NAME?

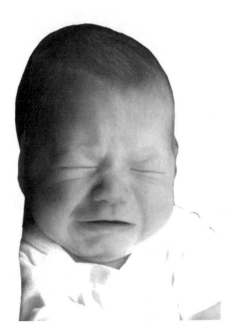

Thirty-third President Harry S. Truman's middle name is just that—"S." After a family feud about whether the new baby should be named after his paternal grandfather, Shippe, or his maternal grandfather, Solomon, Truman's mother threw up her hands and settled with what would please both sides.

Truman wasn't the only president with nominal issues. **President Eisenhower was initially named after his father**, David Dwight Eisenhower. However, the two men tired of being confused with the other, so Eisenhower decided to call himself Dwight David instead.

> George Washington often carried a portable sundial in his pocket.

Lyndon B. Johnson's household didn't strive for clarity between their identities either—the entire family's initials are L.B.J. When Johnson realized his wife, Lady Bird Johnson, bore the same initials, the couple decided to stick with the cheesy trend and name their children likewise: Lynda Bird and Luci Baines.

★ ★ ★ ★ ★

DOLLARS AND SENSE

Not a very trusting woman, Mama Sara Roosevelt never allowed her son (Franklin Delano, that is) to manage the family money. Apparently, she didn't think he was capable of keeping track of the bills. She must have been waiting for his training—years spent presiding over one of the largest fiscal annual budgets on Earth while serving as president from 1933–1945.

As a young man, President James Buchanan was a stickler for a tight budget. His account books included nearly every penny he gave and received throughout his entire life. Even when he was worth more than $200,000 while serving as American Minister to Great Britain, Buchanan kept a careful list of everything he purchased—down to the buttons on his suspenders. In fact, he once refused a $15,000 check from friend Jeremiah Black because it was miswritten by ten cents.

DID YOU KNOW

Eisenhower played football in college and was injured trying to tackle Jim Thorpe.

★ ★ ★ ★ ★

AILMENTS AND MALADIES

Possibly the sickliest president in U.S. history, James Madison suffered a nasty array of medical problems, from hemorrhoids and headaches to bouts of the flu, throughout his life. During the Revolution, Madison's health problems kept him from serving in the Continental Army.

Some early physicians suggested that staying indoors too much would weaken a man's health, so Madison's doctors pleaded with him to spend less time reading and more time strolling about outdoors. However, Madison wasn't one to listen. He often shut himself in a dark room as early as 9:00 a.m. to ward off the bothersome sunlight that provoked his migraines.

The son of a Presbyterian minister, Woodrow Wilson also seemed too plagued by ailments to have any future in politics. He struggled with dyslexia as a child. He also suffered from such severe heartburn that he often pumped water into his stomach to equalize the acid build-up.

However, by the time he was in his late forties, Wilson covered the sickly façade with charm, and he became a shoe-in for the presidency. He had received a Ph.D. from Johns Hopkins University and had authored several acclaimed history books on American politics. He went on to become famous for powerful legislative acts—the Federal Trade Commission Act and the Federal Reserve Act—that helped stabilize the country's desperate financial situation.

fabulous firsts
First left-handed president: James Garfield

★ ★ ★ ★ ★

LAST CALL FOR ALCOHOL

Rumors of Franklin Pierce's excessive drinking darkened his reputation as a senator in the 1830s. His wittiest opponents called him "a hero of many a well-fought bottle." At one point, he seemed to have gotten the problem under control, leaving his Senate seat for a career as a lawyer and joining the Temperance League in New Hampshire.

However, when Pierce became president, he fell off the wagon when a string of bad luck (and wild company) drove him back to the bottle. His son died in a train accident, his marriage fell apart, and he was surrounded by party-animal congressmen who just couldn't wait for a night (or two) on the town.

As a result, Pierce's years as president were plagued with loneliness and criticism. In 1869, he died of stomach inflammation, probably as a result of excessive alcohol consumption.

General Ulysses S. Grant was also known for his love of whiskey, but his heaviest drinking days were on the battlefield. A temperance committee once visited Lincoln and asked him to fire the general because of his nasty rumored addiction.

Noting Grant's widespread fame for winning battles, however, on November 26, 1863, the *New York Herald* reported Lincoln's reply as "I wish some of you would tell me the brand of whiskey that Grant drinks. I would like to send a barrel of it to every one of my other generals." Lincoln claimed the *Herald's* report was anything but accurate and denied ever making the comment.

Zachary Taylor did not vote at all until he was sixty-two years old. Because he was a soldier and moved so frequently, he couldn't establish legal residency and therefore could not even vote for himself when he ran for office.

★ ★ ★ ★ ★

THE FUGITIVE

The son of a laborer and a weaver, a poor couple who owned no land in their home state of North Carolina, **Andrew Johnson was by far the president most praised for turning rags into riches**.

But Johnson nearly ruined his chances of escaping poverty. When he became an apprentice to a tailor, he fled town without finishing the job (apparently he and some friends had thrown rocks at a neighbor's house and were afraid of being arrested).

Fourteen-year-old Johnson eventually begged for his job back, but his pitiful pleas were denied. Johnson honed his skills and moved his family to the Tennessee mountains to open a tailor's shop. Luckily, the business succeeded, and Johnson was able to marry his sixteen-year-old sweetheart, Eliza McCardle, before accepting the pressures of politics and running for governor.

As a teenager, James K. Polk had a gallstone operation without any anesthesia.

HANGMAN HEAVEN

Born in New Jersey, Grover Cleveland made his fame and fortune while serving as the sheriff of Erie County and the mayor of Buffalo, New York, before running for president in 1893. During his tenure as sheriff,

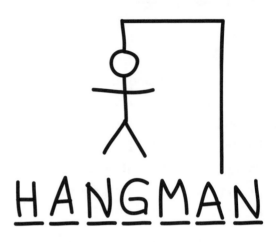

however, he did something no other American president had ever done before (and no future president would ever do)—he personally noosed the necks of a few of Erie County's most infamous criminals.

MEET THE PRESS

Warren Gamaliel Harding edited a blossoming small-town newspaper in Ohio called the *Star*. He loved his job so much that he actually had to be convinced to run for a Senate seat in the early 1900s.

When nineteen-year-old Warren Harding and a few of his friends purchased the *Marion Star* in 1884, the paper was scarcely more than a flyer and had just a few hundred subscribers. Five years later, it had become the most popular newspaper in the county and one of the most successful newspapers in the state.

Compared to the hustle and bustle of daily deadlines, however, politics seemed like a breeze.

Harding once said the only reason he stayed in the Senate for four whole years was that he had become a somewhat famous, respectable "gentleman" overnight and could pay the bills while under less stress than at the *Star*.

A man with very little confidence, Harding acclimated to the lazy days of socialite schmoozing and never dreamt of taking complete responsibility for the U.S. government. His wife, whom he called Duchess, disagreed. She wanted the prestige of living in the White House so badly that she eventually convinced him to campaign. Mrs. Harding thought she knew what was best, but she may have been wrong—while in office, her husband had two quite scandalous affairs with other women.

★ ★ ★ ★ ★

I Can't Get No Respect

The only twentieth-century president not to have a college degree, Harry S. Truman received little respect from his political colleagues. He grew up working as a mail clerk, a bookkeeper, and a farmer. After fighting in World War I, he moved home and opened a men's clothing store in Kansas City, with little success.

Truman took a stab at politics, serving as a judge and a senator for a few years before his party talked him into running for vice president. However, Truman never had the tenacity and confidence to win over his political opponents. In fact, when he arrived at his predecessor's funeral in 1945, no one even stood to acknowledge that he had just become the new commander in chief.

Wary of filling FDR's shoes, Truman worked to earn clout, authorizing the use of atomic bombs against Japan to win World War II. Regardless, no one thought Truman would win reelection because of the country's drastic post-war economic slump.

On Election Day, the *Chicago Daily Tribune* had already printed "DEWEY DEFEATS TRUMAN" on the front page of the following day's paper. Truman won, but he hardly had time to celebrate before the Cold War exploded, a communist dictatorship overtook China, and the Soviet Union started openly constructing atomic bombs.

Unfortunately, the bad luck of Truman's boyhood carried over into his second term—he just couldn't get a break.

★ ★ ★ ★ ★

SIX DEGREES OF PRESIDENTIAL SEPARATION

Some presidents may have been genetically set up for success—many of them were related to each other and to some of the brightest characters in history.

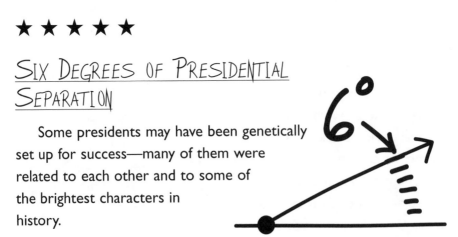

- **George Washington** was James-Madison's half cousin twice removed, Queen Elizabeth II's second cousin seven times removed, Robert E. Lee's third cousin twice removed, and Winston Churchill's very distant cousin.

- **James K. Polk** was a great-grandnephew of John Knox, the founder of the Scottish Presbyterian Church.

- **Theodore Roosevelt** was Martin Van Buren's third cousin twice removed.

- **Grover Cleveland** was Ulysses S. Grant's sixth cousin once removed.

- **Franklin D. Roosevelt** was related to Winston Churchill and to his own wife, Eleanor (a second cousin). He was also related by either blood or marriage to eleven other presidents: John Adams, John Quincy Adams, Ulysses S. Grant, William Henry Harrison, Benjamin Harrison, James Madison, Theodore Roosevelt, William Taft, Zachary Taylor, Martin Van Buren, and George Washington.

- **George W. Bush** is distantly related to Benedict Arnold and Marilyn Monroe. He is also Franklin Pierce's fifth cousin four times removed, Theodore Roosevelt's seventh cousin three times removed, and Abraham Lincoln's seventh cousin four times removed.

> George W. Bush and John Kerry have several cousins in common: Walt Disney, Michael Douglas, Clint Eastwood, the Wright Brothers, Hugh Hefner, Clara Barton, Princess Diana, and Howard Dean.

★ ★ ★ ★ ★

REDSKIN REBELLION

As a young captain serving under General "Mad Anthony" Wayne in the Northwest Territories, **William Henry Harrison proved stalwart against Native Americans** trying to stop white men from pushing west. In fact, he was so ruthless that President Adams made him governor of the Indian Territory (now Indiana and Illinois) to "negotiate" treaties with locals.

However, Harrison's idea of negotiation was a bit askew. He first defeated the tribes in battle, and then forced them to give up their land for pennies on the dollar. He paid one tribe a single cent for each 200 acres of a fifty-one million-acre deal.

Shawnee Chief Tecumseh did everything he could to organize a resistance and prevent the taking of his land by force, but he was killed after teaming up with the British in the War of 1812. As a result of his efforts to squash Native American resistance, Harrison became a national hero.

Years later, **twelfth President Zachary Taylor was also famed as an "Indian fighter,"** but his motives as a soldier were for peace rather than prosperity. Taylor married Margaret Mackall Smith in 1810 and moved his family from military post to post before finally settling in Baton Rouge, Louisiana.

He often protected Native American lands from violent white settlers looking to invade. Taylor longed for peaceful coexistence between the two groups and relied on military involvement to keep both sides at bay. In the end, he was nicknamed "Old Rough and Ready" for his willingness to get his hands dirty and join his troops in battle for the sake of justice.

★ ★ ★ ★ ★

WIN ONE FOR THE GIPPER

Young Ronald Wilson Reagan got his start in the acting world when his mother, a devout follower of the Disciples of Christ, made him take part in short skits at church. The audience's applause was intoxicating, and Reagan couldn't get enough of being the center of attention.

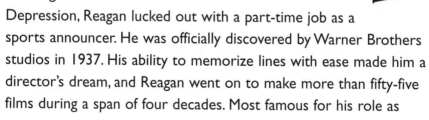

Graduating from college in the height of the Depression, Reagan lucked out with a part-time job as a sports announcer. He was officially discovered by Warner Brothers studios in 1937. His ability to memorize lines with ease made him a director's dream, and Reagan went on to make more than fifty-five films during a span of four decades. Most famous for his role as inspirational Notre Dame football player George Gipp in *Knute Rockne: All American*, Reagan made B-list film audiences swoon for many years.

Despite his romantic roles on the big screen, Reagan surrendered his dreamy ways when it came to his first wife, actress Jane Wyman. The two twisted lovebirds planned their marriage ceremony in Forest Lawn Cemetery in Glendale, California. (It's no wonder he became the first divorced president.)

★ ★ ★ ★ ★

School's Out Forever

Whether as a short-time gig for some extra cash or a term as a university president, more than fourteen American presidents served as educators before or after their time at the White House. But dealing with restless children and belligerent parents weren't their most shining moments in history.

John Adams was the first president to become a teacher when he graduated from Harvard University in 1755 and became Latin master at a grammar school in Worcester, Massachusetts. It didn't take long before Adams was describing his students as "little runtlings, just capable of lisping A, B, C and troubling the master." After only two years of teaching, he fled education and became a lawyer.

Adams wasn't the only president-to-be who sprinted from the classroom to the courtroom. Andrew Jackson taught near his South Carolina hometown but hated it so much that he quit after less than a year to study law. Woodrow Wilson did the opposite—he quit his Atlanta law practice, earned a Ph.D., and went on to serve as a professor for nearly a decade. He taught history and coached football at Bryn Mawr College in Pennsylvania and taught political economy at Princeton University before being elected as president of the university and then president of the United States.

> Ulysses S. Grant was nicknamed "Useless" as a child. His birth name was actually Hiram Ulysses Grant, but he changed it to Ulysses S. after fearing his classmates at West Point would tease him for having the initials H.U.G.

★ ★ ★ ★ ★

EXPULSION 101

It's hard to believe that, after being expelled from his undergrad program as a young college boy in the early 1800s, **James Buchanan wormed his way back into college** and went on to become the fifteenth president.

Hoping his son would one day work alongside him, Buchanan's father sent him to study law at Dickinson College. But after one year, Buchanan senior received a letter saying his son had been kicked out due to "disorderly conduct." The school's president admitted that he would have dismissed Buchanan even sooner if his father weren't so darn respectable. Despite his reputation for drinking, smoking cigars, and taking part in a long list of other rowdy college-boy behaviors, Buchanan cajoled a family friend, who had just become president of the Board of Trustees, into reconsidering. He was granted his wish to re-enroll, and in September 1809, he graduated with a bachelor's degree.

★ ★ ★ ★ ★

School of Spanglish

When he was only twelve years old, **James Madison diligently studied both Spanish and Japanese**. But his language skills later proved painfully inadequate and led to paralyzing embarrassment. While a student at Princeton University, Madison was asked to serve as an interpreter for a French visitor. Madison soon realized he could barely understand what the man was saying. Ultimately, Madison passed the buck, blaming his old Scottish schoolmaster for teaching him a worthless dialect of "Scotch French."

★ ★ ★ ★ ★

White Supremacy Stupidity

Once engaged to the daughter of a Texas Ku Klux Klan leader, Lyndon B. Johnson called off the wedding when he found out that his future father-in-law called his family a bunch of "shiftless dirt farmers and grubby politicians." "None of them will ever amount to a damn," he said, unaware that Johnson would one day become vice president under John F. Kennedy and later the thirty-sixth president of the United States.

★ ★ ★ ★ ★

SMALL-TOWN TINKERING

William McKinley was a simple man with simple beginnings. When he was born in 1843, his small Ohio hometown had "3 churches, 3 stores, 1 blast furnace, rolling mill, nail factory, forge, and about 300 inhabitants," the *Niles-Tribune Chronicle* wrote in 1999.

Several biographers have attributed McKinley's good manners, love of hymns and poetry, and dedication to his often-ill wife to his strong, small-town Methodist upbringing. Originally Scot-Irish Presbyterians, McKinley's parents were often caught up in fiery religious revivals and became Methodists when they moved to Ohio in the early 1800s. After a week of Methodist camp meetings in 1859, young McKinley asked to be baptized.

Although his mother prayed fervently for him to become a minister, the Civil War called him to battle instead. His regiment was devoutly religious and became known as "the psalm singers of the Western Reserve" for their fervent commitment to prayer and preaching. As president, McKinley wrote speeches that often reflected his religious commitments, as they were sprinkled with Christian phrases such as "the Lord most high" and "Him who is sovereign of land and sea."

Aaron Morton, one of McKinley's pastors from back home, said he "was not what you would call a 'shouting Methodist' but rather one who is careful of his acts and words."

★ ★ ★ ★ ★

POP GOES THE PISTOL

Before spending twenty-three years as a soldier, two-year-old Ulysses S. Grant was immune to the loud pop of gunfire. In fact, when a neighbor suggested playing a joke on the young child by firing a pistol nearby, Ulysses's father, Jesse, challenged the man to try it. He even bet that his son would not flinch at the noise. Though the pistol was fired close to the child's head, young Ulysses sang out in amusement, "Fire it again!"

★ ★ ★ ★ ★

SWORN INTO THE SKULLS

Born in 1924 to a wealthy banker named Prescott Bush, **George H.W. Bush went on to become the youngest pilot in the Navy** when he was just eighteen years old. After his plane was shot down during a WWII bombing mission in 1944, Bush returned home to Connecticut and married sweetheart Barbara Pierce, who once said Bush was the first man she ever kissed. The couple had six children (one died of leukemia at just three years old), and Bush enrolled at Yale University. There, he played baseball and became a member of an elite secret society known as Skull and Bones.

★ ★ ★ ★ ★

DITCHIN'

Reflecting on his rebellious childhood, **John Adams once told friends he hated studying Latin grammar** so much that he told his father he would rather do something else. In turn, his father suggested he try "ditching," and made him start digging a ditch in the family meadow. Though sweaty and exhausted by the manual labor, stubborn Adams stuck to his work for two days before laying down his pride and admitting he would, indeed, rather study Latin. For the rest of his life, Adams said the ditching experience played an important role in forming his character.

DID YOU KNOW?

James A. Garfield weighed ten pounds when he was born and was the last president born in a log cabin.

★ ★ ★ ★ ★

RIGHT TO BITE

In the early 1900s, while president of Princeton University, **Woodrow Wilson ran into some roadblocks** when trying to promote intellectual growth among the country's most promising students. He conceived a system of "quadrangles" where students would live, eat, and study with faculty members on campus. Other highbrow institutions, such as Oxford and Cambridge, had been modeling similar programs, but Princeton's existing "fraternity-like eating clubs" refused to be replaced with the new concept. Eventually, the clubs' alumni rebelled, intimidating the school's trustees into dropping the idea.

★ ★ ★ ★ ★

MR. INDEPENDENT

Mature beyond his years, **John Quincy Adams did not feel the need to receive much schooling** before jumping into an early career in diplomatic affairs. At just fourteen years old, he became the private secretary of Francis Dana, the Chief Justice of Massachusetts. He then spent six months traveling in Europe before joining his father's political efforts in Paris. Adams ultimately ditched his daddy's dollars to live in the United States on his own. In his diary, he wrote, "I am determined that so long as I shall be able to get my own living in an honorable manner, I will depend upon no one."

★ ★ ★ ★ ★

HE'S GOT THE BLUES

After graduating from college in the mid-1700s, **James Madison fell into a surprisingly religious funk**. He immersed himself in biblical studies and turned from a lover of poetry and romance to a hard-nosed theologian, reasoning endlessly on the issue of free will. While other Virginia boys were romancing women, racing horses, and wrestling outdoors, Madison delved into the Scriptures, trying to find solutions to the obsessions that plagued him.

Chapter 2

Shaking Hands and Kissing Babies: Moments in Campaign History

JACKSON

Shaking Hands and Kissing Babies: Moments in Campaign History

★ ★ ★ ★ ★ ★ ★ ★ ★ ★ ★ ★ ★ ★ ★ ★ ★

With their lyrical "Tippecanoe and Tyler Too," William Henry Harrison's remarkably cheesy campaign strategy during the 1840 presidential election, the Whigs set the pace with the first campaign slogan ever. Since then, the desperate race to serve as the next commander in chief has led to everything from silly sing-song slogans and ridiculous rhymes to candidates' faces and poetic jingles on flasks and packs of cigarettes. Whether official jargon or simply products loosely associated with the campaign, these strategies are the worst of the worst.

When Andrew Jackson beat out John Quincy Adams in the election of 1828, the town of Adams, New Hampshire, originally named after the latter, changed its name to Jackson.

★ ★ ★ ★ ★

THE KNOW NOTHINGS

In 1849, New York's patriotic partisans formed a **secret society called The Order of the Star Spangled Banner**, which became so popular that just five years later, they had enough members to hold a national convention and nominate a candidate for presidency. However, the group did little to convince Americans that they had the know-how to run the country. Its members were strictly instructed to keep The Order's decisions and happenings secret, so they quickly became known as the "Know Nothing Party."

When asked for details on the party's political plans, members would reply, "I know nothing," and walk away. As ignorant and silly as the pact may have seemed, the appeal of the mystery worked until the group divided on the issue of slavery, and their candidate, former President Millard Fillmore, lost the election miserably.

When John Adams moved his family to Washington to live in the White House, they got lost in the woods for several hours. As they circled, they had no idea that they were just barely north of the city.

★ ★ ★ ★ ★

TIPPECANOE AND TYLER TOO

The first "modern" presidential campaign—one with rallies, slogans, and a slew of advertising—was organized in 1840 by the Whigs, an anti-General Jackson party that adopted its name from the British group opposing the monarchy. The Whigs were desperate to beat Jackson's incumbent, Martin Van Buren, and pulled out all the stops to woo voters. They held public barbecues and bonfires where they passed out cider in log-cabin-shaped bottles to support their candidate, William Henry Harrison.

An acclaimed war hero of the Battle of Tippecanoe in 1840, Harrison and his running mate, John Tyler, wanted to remind America who the bravest candidate on the ballot was with the slogan "Tippecanoe and Tyler Too." "Tippecanoe" referred to the battle in which Harrison and his forces slaughtered Native Americans resisting the western movement of white settlers in the early 1800s.

DID YOU KNOW
Warren G. Harding coined the word "normalcy."

33

Regardless of the disrespect to the deceased, Old Tippecanoe managed to win the race. However, his victory was short-lived, as he died just thirty days after he took office. His grandson, Benjamin, would later carry on his legacy as president in 1889.

★ ★ ★ ★ ★

WHO IS JAMES K. POLK?

With his slogan—**"Who is James K. Polk?"**—Henry Clay tried to assert that no one had ever heard of (and therefore should never vote for) his opponent, the Democratic Party's nominee for president. But Clay's strategy backfired and may have actually imprinted Polk's name into voters' minds. The Democrats had deadlocked on other options for the candidacy and probably expected their "dark horse" to lose miserably, but Polk surprised them with a win.

★ ★ ★ ★ ★

THE CONTINENTAL LIAR FROM THE STATE OF MAINE

Grover Cleveland also thought he would slander his political opponent with a catchy slogan leading up to his 1884 election. Aware of some unethical investments and business deals Republican James G. Blaine had allegedly made during his career in the railroad industry, he came up with the sing-song "Blaine, Blaine, James G. Blaine—The Continental Liar from the State of Maine." While it sounds like a childish rhyme a group of six-year-old girls might sing while skipping rope, the slogan worked, and Cleveland sailed into office.

> "Sensible and responsible women do not want to vote."
> —Grover Cleveland

Blaine may have lost miserably, but he wasn't going down without a fight. He retaliated with his own jingle, taunting Cleveland for the out-of-wedlock child he was accused of having fathered before the election: "Ma, Ma, Where's My Pa ... Gone to the White House, Ha, Ha, Ha." Apparently America saw right through the raw rivalry and opted for a womanizer over a cheating businessman.

The turning point in this dirty mudslinging contest came when a Blaine supporter, Protestant minister Samuel Burchard, announced that Democrats were a party of "rum, Romanism, and rebellion." While Blaine could have stepped up and disassociated himself with the comments, he chose to stay out of the rumor mill. However, he was quickly tied to the minister's tirade, as the public assumed he, too, thought urban immigrants were "drunkards, followers of the pope, and the cause of the Civil War." Of course, Blaine lost his appeal to Irish voters, and Cleveland won by twenty thousand votes.

★ ★ ★ ★ ★

COX AND COCKTAILS

When James Cox announced his opposition to Prohibition just before he ran for president in the early 1920s, his opponent, Warren G. Harding, made up a catchphrase to paint him as a dark drunk with the slogan "Cox and Cocktails." Rather than conjuring up fond memories of college keg parties, the slogan worked, and Harding eased into his first term.

Cox wasn't the only presidential candidate to suffer from an anti-Prohibition stance. In 1928, New York Governor Alfred E. Smith was running against Herbert Hoover when it came down to influential Josiah William Bailey and Methodist Bishop James Cannon to influence voters nationwide. Bailey supported Democratic candidate Smith, while Cannon—an ardent Prohibitionist—was an energetic leader in the fight against him.

DID YOU KNOW

James Madison's inaugural address contained one seemingly endless sentence that was 376 words long.

★ ★ ★ ★ ★

ANYONE BUT PIERCE

It's one thing to be jeered at and slandered by your opponent's campaign, but **when your own party turns against you** and begs America not to vote for you, you know the strategy has gone south. In 1857, Democrat Franklin Pierce experienced this unfortunate scenario firsthand. His own party unofficially changed its slogan to "Anyone But Pierce." Understandably, the fourteenth president abandoned all hope for reelection.

★ ★ ★ ★ ★

PUT YOUR MONEY WHERE YOUR FAITH IS

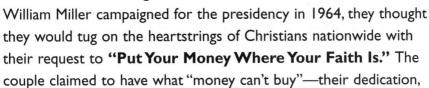

When Republican Barry Goldwater and running mate William Miller campaigned for the presidency in 1964, they thought they would tug on the heartstrings of Christians nationwide with their request to **"Put Your Money Where Your Faith Is."** The couple claimed to have what "money can't buy"—their dedication, determination, and strong religious faith.

After they convinced America they were trustworthy men of God, they started pleading for pocket change to go not

> "I just won't get into a pissing contest with that skunk."
>
> —Dwight Eisenhower, referring to Senator Joe McCarthy

into the collection plate but toward their campaign, so they could fund what money can buy—television time, billboards, and newspaper ads.

★ ★ ★ ★ ★

VOTE YOURSELF A FARM

In 1860, the **Republican Party and its shoe-in presidential candidate, Abraham Lincoln**, decided to play on the sympathies of a country thirsty for the quick money of the American Dream. In hopes that their "Vote Yourself A Farm" campaign paid off (literally), Lincoln and his associates promised to pass a law granting free land to anyone who moved their family out west.

But Lincoln didn't pioneer the concept. One widely distributed handbill from 1848, twelve years before Lincoln ran for president, read:

"Are you an American citizen? Then you are a joint owner of the public lands. Why not take enough of your property to provide yourself a home? Why not vote yourself a farm?

"Are you a party follower? Then you have long enough employed your vote to benefit scheming office seekers. Use it for once to benefit yourself: Vote yourself a farm.

"Are you tired of slavery? Of drudging for others? Of poverty and its attendant miseries? Then vote yourself a farm."

THE BULL MOOSE BLUES

"I want to be a Bull Moose
And with the Bull Moose stand
With Antlers on my forehead
And a Big Stick in my hand."
—Bull Moose Party jingle

Yankee Doodle Went to Vote

Most of the cheesy (yet effective) campaign songs were parodies of popular American favorites, such as "Battle Cry of Freedom" and "John Brown's Body." Alfred Wheeler wrote the following tune for Zachary Taylor's 1848 campaign:

(sung to the tune of "Yankee Doodle")

> We'll sing a song to suit the times,
> With voices bold and steady,
> And cheerily we'll tell in rhymes
> Of good old Rough and Ready.
> His foes may slander as they can,
> And bluster at his manners,
> Who cares a fig? He's just the man
> To lead the Yankee banners.
>
> Chorus:
> Then Rough and Ready let it ring,
> And set the bells a chiming,
> Where'er we go we're bound to sing
> His praises in our rhyming.
>
> In Florida he gained a name
> That won our admiration,
> And loudly has his gallant fame
> Been echoed thro' the nation.

There's not a heart in all the land,
That beats not firm and steady,
For the hero of the Rio Grande,
Old gallant Rough and Ready.

★ ★ ★ ★ ★

A FULL DINNER PAIL

When William McKinley campaigned for the presidency in 1900, he hoped **to win the hearts of the American public by passing out stamped metal dinner pails.** The hokey, but brilliant, scheme reminded voters of the country's prosperity during McKinley's first term as president. He won, but his second term came to an early, tragic end when he was assassinated at the Buffalo Pan-American Exposition in September 1901.

FDR served hot dogs to the King and Queen of England when they came to the White House for a visit

★ ★ ★ ★ ★

A CHICKEN IN EVERY POT AND A CAR IN EVERY GARAGE

Talking his fellow countrymen into the notion that they would be economically sound and secure if he were president in 1928, Herbert Hoover told voters that they would have **"a chicken in every pot and a car in every garage."** Little did he know that his staff would face the worst depression the country had ever seen.

41

★ ★ ★ ★ ★

Not Just Peanuts

Jimmy Carter may have made a fortune working on the family peanut farm in Georgia, but he had other qualifications, too. During his campaign, Carter felt the need to plead with America (inconspicuously, of course) to consider the fact that he did have talents other than the ones related to his homegrown farmer-boy image. He passed out a T-shirt featuring his face and the line "Not Just Peanuts" to prove his point.

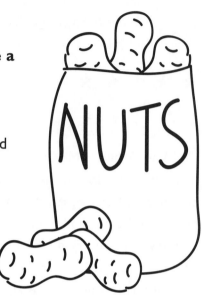

★ ★ ★ ★ ★

Cheesy Memorabilia: The Early Years

Political campaigns have always meant freebie trinkets for those willing to stock their closets and put old items on eBay. Some historians say Andrew Jackson was the first presidential candidate to organize and distribute campaign memorabilia. However, most associate the diversity of mass-produced junk with William Henry Harrison's "Log Cabin" crusade. Aside from the ever-present lapel button, which made its appearance in the 1896 McKinley/Bryan election, tacky collectibles have included everything from paperweights and potholders to coffee mugs and pocket combs.

In 1945, the nonprofit organization American Political Items Collectors was founded "to encourage the collection, preservation, and study of political Americana." Today, the group has three thousand dedicated members (with too much time on their hands), including former Presidents Bill Clinton and Jimmy Carter. In honor of history buffs and trinket geeks alike, it is important to pay tribute to some of the strange, often desperate, attempts to win over the American public with stickers, beer mugs, and more.

★ ★ ★ ★ ★

SMOKIN' SAMUEL TILDEN

In the 1870s, Democratic candidate (and Governor) **Samuel Jones Tilden of New York teamed with Blackwell Durham Bull Tobacco Company** to print a round of advertisements pushing what would be his failed run for the presidency. On the front of the card was Tilden's face. As the card opened, it transformed into President Ulysses S. Grant, a Republican from Ohio who had served the term before and did not run in 1876. Tilden hoped to appeal to both political parties with the card, but his choice to campaign on a cigarette box just didn't pay off. The Republicans barely won the election, and Rutherford B. Hayes took office.

The card read:

> Come all you true born Democrats,
> You hardy hearts of oak,
> Who know a thing when it is good
> And Blackwell's Durham smoke.
> Gaze on this face and you will see
> Your presidential nominee
> The sage and statesman S.J.T.
> And all you good Republicans
> Will surely be enchanted
> When you behold the visage here
> And take the fact for granted
> That he will win if he will be
> Your presidential nominee
> The soldier, hero, U.S.G.
>
> But though you differ in your views
> Political, we hope
> You coincide when we remark
> The choicest brand to smoke
> Is Blackwell's Genuine Durham that
> Suits every taste no matter what,
> Republican or Democrat.

★ ★ ★ ★ ★

DRINKING DAYS ARE HERE AGAIN

Before smoking and drinking became today's health taboo, many candidates chose to win voters' hearts with tobacco and alcohol. Some passed out whiskey bottles. After Prohibition was repealed, FDR passed out shot glasses that read, "Happy Days Are Here Again." Tobacco-related campaign giveaways originated with free snuffboxes during early nineteenth-century elections. In the 1950s, Ike passed around cigarettes by the dozen, and in the 1950s, candidate Adlai Stevenson actually pasted his own face on a pack of cigarettes. In 1972, Nixon campaigned with bubblegum cigars.

Although George Washington was one of the wealthiest men in America, he had to borrow money to attend his own inauguration. His wealth was attributed to his vast amounts of property, but he had very little cash.

> "What is the use of being president if you can't have a train with a diner on it?"
> —William Howard Taft

Chapter 3

Fact and Fiction: Debunking Myths and Legends

Fact and Fiction: Debunking Myths and Legends

Elvis was abducted by aliens, and the scary man with the hook knows what you did last summer. Well, not quite. American history is sprinkled with a ridiculous list of mind-boggling myths. From the origin of the seventh-inning stretch to the humble log-cabin beginnings of some of our favorite commanders in chief, one wonders if the history books ever get it right. The lavish, trend-setting lives of the American presidents are no different, yet so many history buffs tell tales that, well, never actually happened.

> William Taft was the tubbiest commander in chief to ever hold office. Maybe he should have cut back on the cheese.

★ ★ ★ ★ ★

MYTH 1 · THE SEVENTH-INNING STRETCH

Taft is credited with accidentally instigating a major baseball tradition—the seventh-inning stretch. Apparently, as a game between the Washington Senators and the Philadelphia Athletics dragged on, he became quite restless in his small, wooden stadium chair and got up to stretch his legs in the middle of the seventh inning. Seeing their president rise to his feet, the crowd stood to show its respect. When Taft sat down a few minutes

> "I'm not going to have some reporters pawing through our papers. We are the president."
> —Hillary Clinton

later, everyone else in the stadium followed his lead and the game continued. Unfortunately, the tale is nothing more than folklore.

On April 14, 1910, Taft did become the first president to throw the first pitch commemorating the baseball season's opening day. The Senators and the Athletics were warming up at Griffith Stadium when, at the last minute, umpire Billy Evans tossed Taft the game ball and asked him to give it a throw toward home plate. Every president since—except Jimmy Carter—has opened at least one season.

Taft is not the only man credited with having inspired this baseball tradition. Some say Brother Jasper of Manhattan College invented it in the late 1800s. Others credit Harry Wright of the Cincinnati Red Stockings. Historians claim to have uncovered an 1869 letter in which Wright observed that baseball fans naturally tend to mill about during the seventh inning. Ultimately, very little evidence remains that Taft was the first to practice it.

fabulous firsts
First president to ride on a steamboat: James Monroe

★ ★ ★ ★ ★

Myth 2 · Writing On Rubbish

Most children learn that **Abraham Lincoln penned his famous Gettysburg Address on the back of an envelope** while traveling on a train. While the story is inspiring (and impressive, considering how bumpy railroads were in the 1860s), records at The Lincoln Museum in Fort Wayne, Indiana, suggest otherwise. They show that Lincoln worked on the address both before and after his train ride from Washington, D.C., to Gettysburg. And he used official stationery, not an old scrap of envelope, for the first handwritten draft.

★ ★ ★ ★ ★

MYTH 3 · IT'S A FARMER'S LIFE FOR THEE

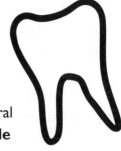

> "Solutions are not the answer."
> —Richard Nixon

American history hails the tale of the heartless liberals who once told Native Americans to **join the culture of white men and learn how to farm or die**. In 1808, Thomas Jefferson did tell the Delewares to "begin every man a farm, let him enclose it, cultivate it, build a warm house on it, and when he dies let it belong to his wife and children after him."

However, author James W. Loewen says legislation had been passed in at least one state that would punish anyone who taught Native Americans how to read and write. And as for teaching them how to farm, Native Americans in many states already lived a life of agriculture. Regardless of what the history books may say, Loewen believes conflict was inevitable.

★ ★ ★ ★ ★

MYTH 4 · THE WHOLE TOOTH AND NOTHING BUT THE TOOTH

While it is true that at his inauguration President George Washington only had one natural tooth, **his dentures were never actually made**

of wood. Nor were they made by Paul Revere, as many legends proclaim. Washington did go through several pairs of choppers, but they were made out of lead and human or animal teeth. In fact, his inauguration speech—only 183 words long—took a whole ninety seconds to read because the dentures were so cumbersome.

Elementary-school lessons aside, Washington also never chopped down a cherry tree. And he never threw a dollar across the Potomac River. Where did all these myths originate? They most likely made their first appearance in the book *A History of the Life and Death, Virtues, and Exploits of General George Washington*, which was published by a parson named Mason Locke Weems just after Washington's death. Washington was larger than life to his admirers, and that's just how Weems wanted to portray him.

fabulous firsts

First president to ride in an automobile to his own inauguration: Warren G. Harding

One of Weems's fabrications about George Washington's life, however, still persists at Valley Forge National Historic Park. In the popular, beautiful Washington Memorial Chapel, a stunning stained glass window portrays General Washington kneeling in prayer. A National Historic

Park pamphlet explains that the image commemorates a moment of humility as Washington sought God's guidance at a desperate time of war. The same image of the kneeling general is displayed in bronze statues at the Pennsylvania Freedom Foundation and in a painting at the Valley Forge Historical Society museum. In a magazine article in 1804, Weems wrote, "while Washington ... lay encamped at Valley Forge, a certain good old friend, of the respectable family name of Potts ... had occasion to pass through the woods near headquarters. Treading his way along the venerable grove, suddenly he heard the sound of a human voice ... [it was] the commander in chief of the American armies on his knees in prayer!"

Despite the story's romanticism, historian Paul F. Boller Jr. insists the fable is completely false. The man by the name of Potts who Weems claimed saw Washington was certainly not near the forge in that winter of 1777. Regardless, the myth lives on—in 1928, the United States Postal Service issued a two-cent stamp, displaying Washington on his knees, in honor of the battle at Valley Forge's 150th anniversary.

> "If it takes the entire army and navy of the United States to deliver a postcard in Chicago, that card will be delivered."
> —Grover Cleveland

THE LINCOLN-KENNEDY COINCIDENCES

While some think the strange-but-true links between Abraham Lincoln and John F. Kennedy are incredible, others are skeptical. Freaky but historically true, is this timeline a twilight-zone trick or simply a coincidence? You be the judge.

- Lincoln was elected to Congress in 1846.

- Kennedy was elected to Congress in 1946.

- Lincoln was elected president in 1860.

- Kennedy was elected president in 1960.

- The names Lincoln and Kennedy both contain seven letters.

- Both lost their children while living in the White House.

- Both were shot with one bullet, in the head, on a Friday.

- Lincoln was shot in Ford Theatre.

- Kennedy was shot in a Ford Lincoln vehicle.

- Lincoln's secretary was named Kennedy.

- Kennedy's secretary was named Lincoln.

- Both men's successors were named Johnson. Andrew Johnson was born in 1808. Lyndon Johnson was born in 1908.

- John Wilkes Booth, who assassinated Lincoln, was born in 1839.

- Lee Harvey Oswald, who assassinated Kennedy, was born in 1939.

- Booth ran from the theater and was caught in a warehouse. Oswald ran from a warehouse and was caught in a theater.

- Both assassins were assassinated before their trials.

★ ★ ★ ★ ★

Myth 5 · Bathtub History Bluff

In 1917, a writer named **H.L. Mencken published a startling account of America's love affair with the bathtub** in the *New York Evening Mail.* An obvious crock, his tale was written off the top of his creative little journalistic head—but the public believed every word. In the article, Mencken notes that physicians across the nation believed bathtubs to be a serious health danger. At one point, he writes that legislators in Boston and Philadelphia tried to pass laws against owning them, but he writes that opposition to bathing sitting down ended in 1851, when Millard Fillmore had a tub installed in the White House. If the president could have one, then the people could too.

Shocked (and amused) that his lie had become a part of American history, Mencken remained silent for ten years while his story grew roots and became household trivia. In May 1926, he finally publicly admitted that his article was fabricated and that he never expected such widespread acceptance (and so little fact checking). Regardless, the article was published again, just a few months after his confession, in *Scribner's Magazine.* In the 1930s, a book was written on his theory. The madness doesn't stop there—in the 1970s, Mencken's spoof was even published in the *Dictionary of American History.*

Myth 6 · Deaf Man Walking

If you've ever seen the Lincoln Memorial, it's hard to deny that the hands on **the giant stone statue seem to be posed in the American Sign Language symbols for the letters "A" and "L."** However, the daughter of sculptor Daniel Chester French insists that molding the president's initials was not her father's intent. French claimed to have modeled his work after casts of both Lincoln's hands and his own hands. Thus, there is no secret message communicated through the memorial. Some suspicious history buffs claim that the face of Lincoln's greatest nemesis, Confederate leader Robert E. Lee, was secretly carved into the back of the statue. That, too, is a myth.

Myth 7 · The Pilfered Cadaver

Panic-stricken Lincoln fanatics can breathe a sigh of relief: His corpse was never stolen by a band of thrill-seeking thieves. Between 1865 and 1871, Lincoln's body was kept in a receiving vault, then in a vault at Springfield's Oak Ridge Cemetery, before being transferred to the official Lincoln Tomb in 1871. There was a plot to steal the body eleven years after Lincoln's death, but the 1876 attempt to steal it and hold it for ransom was thwarted by officials before the theft could be pulled off. When the tomb was rebuilt three decades later, it was covered with several feet of concrete to prevent bandits from dreaming of a burglary.

★ ★ ★ ★ ★

MYTH 8 · THE FLATULENT STEED

In November 2003, the Internet was rife with e-mails circulating the story of **President George W. Bush and his stinky carriage ride** from an airport in Great Britain to Buckingham Palace with Queen Elizabeth II. After riding in a 1934 Bentley to Central London, Bush and Her Majesty boarded a magnificent seventeenth-century coach pulled by six stunning white horses, the e-mail read. "Suddenly the scene was shattered when the right rear horse let rip the most horrendous, earth-shattering, eye-smarting blast of flatulence, and the coach filled with noxious fumes." Apparently, the two managed to keep their cool until the Queen apologized for the incident. Bush, confused, thought she was admitting to being the source of the dizzying stench.

While Bush did make a formal visit to England and dine with Queen Elizabeth II in November 2003, the story about the carriage ride is mere imaginative Internet banter. The joke, writes a reporter for a popular urban legend website, is an old one. Through the years,

SLANG OF THE UNION

While some doubt that the phrase "It's OK." originated with Martin Van Buren, the legend is true. Van Buren grew up in Kinderhook, New York, and became known as "Old Kinderhook" when he first got involved in politics. When asking for him, his associates would say, "Is it O.K.?" The phrase stuck and has been carried through more than 150 years of slang ever since.

variations of the story have been told, placing the Prime Minister of Canada, the Archbishop of Canterbury, and a slew of other bigwigs in the protagonist's smelly seat. One Internet version even makes Ronald Reagan and Bush's forerunner Bill Clinton the subject of the tall tale. The earliest version, however, may have been in the 1972 novel *Post Cabin*, by Patrick O'Brian.

★ ★ ★ ★ ★

Myth 9 · The Real First President

While the most widely accepted historical accounts name George Washington as the first official president of the United States, it is not exactly true. Some say **John Hanson, Maryland's representative at the Continental Congress, was the first true leader of the nation**. On November 5, 1781, he was elected by his associates as the "President of the United States in Congress Assembled" and served for one year. Two other men served before him, but he was the first to use the title. Seven other leaders succeeded him before Washington was elected.

★ ★ ★ ★ ★

Myth 10 · Jefferson Mis-Remembered

The Jefferson Memorial in Washington, D.C., presents the writings of Thomas Jefferson so that sightseers can reflect on the third president's infinite wisdom. Most visitors don't know, however, that the Jefferson Memorial rearranges several quotes and therefore (according to some historians) misrepresents Jefferson's original message and ideals.

For example, one panel leaves out five words of the preamble and conclusion of the Declaration of Independence. The fantastic fumble was purposeful, as the architect who built the memorial thought it would make the carefully etched phrases fit better on the display.

On another panel, which displays Jefferson's thoughts on religious freedom, the memorial first presents three quotations from Jefferson's "Act for Religious Freedom" and then adds to the end a random fourth sentence that was not a part of the Act at all—it is from a letter he wrote to James Madison ten years later. The sentence reads, "I know but one code of morality for men whether acting singly or collectively." However, in this sentence, Jefferson was not talking about religion at all—he and Madison were corresponding about the economy.

★ ★ ★ ★ ★

MYTH 11 · ROUGH RIDERS REDEEMED

Teddy Roosevelt has long been famous for leading his Rough Riders up San Juan Hill during the Spanish-American

War's Battle of San Juan. However, they actually charged up nearby Kettle Hill—a smaller mound of land to the right of famous San Juan. By the time Teddy and gang ascended and descended Kettle Hill and followed the rest of the American troops up San Juan Hill, the Spanish fleet was long gone, having fled in surrender. Regardless, the Rough Riders were so popular with the American public that when Roosevelt ran for governor of New York in 1898, he had several former soldiers dress in their military garb and campaign alongside the president-to-be.

★ ★ ★ ★ ★

Myth 12 · Log Cabin Lies: Part 1

William Henry Harrison did not live up to the rumors of his log-cabin birth. Instead, he was born in a brick mansion on a wealthy plantation along the James River. The log-cabin myth actually came about during Harrison's 1840 campaign for presidency, when a newspaper accused him of wanting nothing more out of life than a "pension, plenty of hard cider, and a log cabin." Instead of taking the comment as an insult, the Whigs took advantage of the mockery and presented their candidate as a humble, simple man with a small-town background to which any man

could relate. Harrison never validated the rumor that he was born in a log cabin, but to uphold his image, he never denied it, either.

★ ★ ★ ★ ★

Myth 13 · Log Cabin Lies: Part 2

Lincoln is rumored to have been born in a small cabin on Sinking Spring Farm near Hodgenville, Kentucky, in February 1809. However, by the time Lincoln was assassinated, the cabin seemed to have disappeared. It may have burned down, or neighbors could have torn it apart to use the wood for their own construction efforts.

In 1895, two men, Alfred Dennett and Rev. James Bigham, bought the Lincoln family's farmland, built their own cabin on the property, and tried to pass it off to tourists as the actual building in which Lincoln was born. Fortunately, few passersby made the trip to tour their "historic" hoax, but Bigham wasn't through with his scheming. If the tourists wouldn't come to them, they would go to the tourists. They took the cabin apart and reassembled it at the 1897 Tennessee Centennial Exposition in Nashville and the 1901 Pan-American Exposition in Buffalo.

Eventually, magazine publisher Robert Collier bought the Hodgenville farm and the logs from the so-called Lincoln Cabin (for a whopping $1,000) and shipped them back to Kentucky—stopping the train in a few cities along the way so people could pay to touch them for good luck.

Although it was honest about the building's true beginnings for a time, today the Park Service in Hodgenville claims the "Traditional Lincoln Birthplace Cabin" is real (and even prohibits visitors from using flash photography for fear it could damage the sacred logs). In his book *Lies Across America*, myth-buster James W. Loewen reports that the National Park Service brochure "Abraham Lincoln Birthplace" does say, "because its early history is obscure, there is

fabulous firsts

First senator to become president: James Monroe

lack of documentation to support to authenticity of the cabin," but many other sources cite its absolute validity.

★ ★ ★ ★ ★

MYTH 14 · THE NAKED TRUTH

A typo in The Washington Post made Woodrow Wilson the object of America's gruesome gossip mill when a reporter described his evening out at the theater with new fiancée Edith Galt in 1915. Despite the article's report that "the president spent most of his time entering Mrs. Galt" that evening, rumors that the two lovebirds were getting it on in the back row were completely untrue. The reporter meant to write that "the president spent most of his time entertaining Mrs. Galt."

That press error wasn't the only terrible mix-up suffered by a president, however. After his inauguration in 1901, Teddy Roosevelt suffered the fallout from a similar spell-check mistake when a New York reporter writing on the occasion accidentally misspelled the word "oath" in the article. Instead of an "o," he printed a "b," and his report read, "For sheer democratic dignity, nothing could exceed the moment when, surrounded by the cabinet and a few distinguished citizens, Mr. Roosevelt took his simple bath, as President of the United States." Talk about a revealing mix-up.

Chapter 4

Red-handed and Pants Down: White House Bad Boys on Their Worst Behavior

HOOVER

Red-handed and Pants Down: White House Bad Boys on Their Worst Behavior

★ ★ ★ ★ ★ ★ ★ ★ ★ ★ ★ ★ ★ ★ ★ ★

Kissing babies and decreasing the country's deficit are all well and good when it comes to improving the future (and the image) of America, but the tantalizing secrets of the presidents' private lives are much more interesting. While busy charming voters, each man had a few skeletons in his closet. Some commanders in chief were abhorrent whiners, while others dodged rumors of adultery. Some cursed the press, while others skirted nasty run-ins with the law. From spitting on the White House carpets to embarrassing America abroad, these moments of presidential misbehavior made for some of the White House's greatest public relations nightmares.

> John Tyler became the only former president named a sworn enemy of the United States when he joined the Confederacy twenty years after his term ended in 1845.

★ ★ ★ ★ ★

SEXUAL HEALING

Bill Clinton may have been the most recent U.S. president to shame his family name with a romp around the White House, but sex scandals are not new to the Oval Office.

In 1802, rumors of Thomas Jefferson's alleged rendezvous with slave Sally Hemings were widely published in capital newspapers, but historians tend to dismiss the accusations as nothing more than rumors.

Ten years before Grover Cleveland became president in 1885, a store clerk named Maria publicly named him as the father of her illegitimate son. Cleveland did not deny the claim, but he kept quiet until the press dug up the truth during his campaign years later. Cleveland's opponents used his dirty little secret against him, taunting him with the rhyme "Ma, ma, where's my pa? Gone to the White House, ha, ha, ha!"

Twenty-ninth President Warren G. Harding was also no stranger to paternity problems. Known as quite the ladies' man, he fathered a child out of wedlock in 1919 while he served in the Senate. Despite public knowledge of the relationship, it continued throughout his presidency. After Harding's death in 1923, his mistress got rich off the juicy details printed in her best-selling book, *The President's Daughter*.

★ ★ ★ ★ ★

STRAIGHT FROM THE AP (ANNOYING PRESS, THAT IS)

Lyndon B. Johnson wasn't going to put up with any crap from nosy members of the press looking to pry into his personal life and political agenda. When a reporter once asked a question Johnson didn't feel like answering, he replied, "Why do you come and ask me, the leader of the Western world, a chicken-shit question like that?"

> # DID YOU KNOW
> At twenty-four, Warren G. Harding suffered a nervous breakdown and spent several weeks in a sanitarium in Battle Creek, Michigan.

Johnson was known to be crass in all areas of his life, however—not just with the media. He would belch, curse, and throw back whiskey in front of guests at his ranch in Texas. He also was known for his way with words and often remarked, "I never trust a man unless I've got his pecker in my pocket."

Ronald Reagan may not have used such colorful language at home or at press conferences, but he did have his own tactics for avoiding nosy reporters. He would often take their questions on the White House lawn with his helicopter roaring in the background, which distorted his voice and left interviewers straining to hear his replies.

★ ★ ★ ★ ★

DUELING DUDES

Although famed as a gentle, self-controlled leader, Abraham Lincoln accepted Democrat James Shields's challenge to a duel in 1842. Angry that Lincoln had written a series of anonymous letters mocking him in the *Sangamo Journal*, Shields wanted his revenge. Lincoln proposed they fight in a 10-by-12-foot square with "cavalry broad swords of the largest size." Being much shorter than Lincoln, the standards put Shields at quite a disadvantage, but he was prepared to fight to the death. Luckily, the two men stalled long enough for friends to arrange a peaceful settlement before the duel ever took place. Both men walked away with nothing more than hurt pride.

★ ★ ★ ★ ★

SLAVE-HATER HYPOCRITE

Thomas Jefferson's original version of the Declaration of Independence actually incorporated a clause to abolish slavery, condemning it as abhorrent, but the Continental Congress disagreed and removed the phrasing from the final draft. While Jefferson was an outspoken opponent of slavery all of his life, no one really understood his passionate (and hypocritical) stance—Jefferson's personal estate housed and was run by more slaves than nearly any other estate in the nation.

Historians can only speculate as to why Jefferson thought he needed hundreds of slaves. Even with so much help, Jefferson had serious financial problems most of his life. He was more than $100,000 in debt by the time he died in 1826.

★ ★ ★ ★ ★

BOYS WILL BE BOYS

Andrew Jackson was quite the man's man when it came to bad habits. In an attempt to make his love for chewing tobacco less revolting, he bought a handful of spittoons for the East Room of the White House. While some complained Jackson was wasting government money, others acknowledged that the

president's nasty spitting could ruin the expensive carpets (and gross out guests). And Jackson wasn't the only president to have a tantalizing taste for tobacco.

John F. Kennedy loved the smell and taste of Cuban cigars so much that he commissioned a friend to buy and stockpile 1,500 premium Havanas just before the signing of the Cuban Trade Embargo, legislation that would have prevented him from buying his beloved stogies in the future.

Franklin Delano Roosevelt was also a sucker for a smoke. Although his doctors urged him to quit smoking, a long cigarette dangling from his lips became his trademark look.

All stories of White House smoking and spitting aside, **no president lit up more than Ulysses S. Grant.** While some thought his horrible drinking habit would lead to his death, the more likely cause was his love affair with the cigar. Grant rarely was seen without one in his mouth, and his adoring public contributed to his addiction. After Grant's victory at Fort Donelson on February 16, 1862, admirers sent him more than ten thousand boxes of cigars. Perhaps the attempt to smoke them all led to his death from throat cancer in 1885.

> "You know, if I were a single man, I might ask that mummy out. That's a good-looking mummy."
> —Bill Clinton, admiring an Inca mummy named Juanita

★ ★ ★ ★ ★

 DO AS I SAY, NOT AS I DO

For a president serving at the peak of Prohibition in the 1930s, Herbert Hoover was a pro at finding the legislation's loopholes (and the nearest watering holes). He would often visit the Belgian Embassy in Washington, D.C., for cocktails. Because the building was considered foreign soil, all libations served there were perfectly legal.

★ ★ ★ ★ ★

Praying Playboy

Jimmy Carter was open about his religious duties during his presidency, often juggling cabinet meetings with Bible studies and teaching Sunday School at First Baptist Church in Washington, D.C. For some reason, however, the evangelical Christian agreed to an interview with *Playboy* in 1976.

In his discussion with the reporter, Carter admitted that he had lust in his heart and, from time to time, felt attracted to other women. "I've looked at a lot of women with lust," he said. "This is something that God recognizes I will do ... and God forgives me for it." His confession was shocking to some but amusing to others, who were happy to see the human side of their president. Carter was quick to tell his interviewer that he was shamed by this fatal attraction and felt it was as bad as if he actually had cheated on his poor wife, Rosalynn.

★ ★ ★ ★ ★

Silence of the Man

Not a man of many words, Calvin Coolidge was nicknamed "Silent Cal" by some. He was once so rudely quiet at his own White House dinner party that a female guest made a bet that she could get him to say more than two words. Upon hearing about the wager, the president looked her in the eyes and said, "You lose." Coolidge and his family were often so discreet about the conversations they did have in public that they would use sign language so as not to be overheard. "If you don't say anything, you won't be called on to repeat it," Coolidge said.

★ ★ ★ ★ ★

Hanky Panky

Republican President William McKinley wasn't much help when it came to his wife's medical woes. Though journalists tried to protect her integrity by rarely writing about her health, First Lady Ida was an epileptic. She often had untimely seizures at public political gatherings, speeches,

Some say the term "the big cheese" originated when Thomas Jefferson was given a 1,235-pound chunk of cheese.

and dinners—in the middle of which her not-so-charming husband would simply place his handkerchief over her face until the embarrassing episode subsided. Although it seemed ridiculously disrespectful at the time, the couple was actually known for being publicly loving. McKinley claimed the darkness of his hanky helped calm his wife's episodes.

PR FOR THE POTTY MOUTHS

While dishing out moral codes as a general, George Washington decided to clean up the dirty language raging on the battlefield to create a more honorable image for the U.S. army. To that end, he issued an order that forbade soldiers from swearing.

EPICUREAN ETIQUETTE

As America came into its own and the country's etiquette shifted away from prim and proper English traditions, **Thomas Jefferson became the first president to shake hands rather than bow** to his respected visitors. His patience was tested, however, after he was sworn into the presidency in 1801. When he returned to his boarding house for dinner, he found the place packed. Every seat was filled, and no one rose to offer a seat to the nation's newest leader. Eventually, a Kentucky senator's wife stood up for him, but Jefferson—never one to dethrone a lady—politely declined.

Jefferson's table manners, on the other hand, were often hardly up to par. He was known to let his pet mockingbird, Dick, perch on his shoulder throughout the day and eat bits of food directly out of his mouth at the dinner table.

★ ★ ★ ★ ★

Vulgar Veggies

Regardless of any charm President George H.W. Bush may have communicated on camera, he was less polite while dining, both at home and in public. He refused to eat broccoli, pitching a little fit

and saying, "I am the President of the United States, and I don't have to eat it!" Southern vegetable farmers were so upset at his pronouncement that they delivered truckloads of broccoli to the White House in protest.

★ ★ ★ ★ ★

Culture Shock

Bush's faux pas extended beyond the dinner table. In January 1992, he drove through Australia holding up to the crow what he thought was a universal symbol for "victory." Unfortunately, no one bothered to tell the president, who had just told the press that he was an expert at global hand gestures, that the "V" he was forming with his fingers was tantamount to flashing the middle finger in the United States. By the time Aussie demonstrators returned the symbol to Bush and chanted their disdain for American leadership, it was simply too late for apologies.

DID YOU KNOW
McKinley could shake hands at the rate of 2,500 per hour.

The following term, **Bill Clinton suffered similar cross-cultural woes** when he wrote a letter to the Romanian government, thanking them for the lovely poncho they had given him after his most recent trip to their country. Confused, government officials had to explain to Clinton that what they had given him was not a poncho but a Romanian flag. The center of the flag, which used to bear the symbol of communism, had been cut out after the country overthrew the previous communist regime. Clinton assumed the hole was for his head.

CLINTON

> "Our enemies are innovative and resourceful, and so are we. They never stop thinking about new ways to harm our country and our people, and neither do we."
>
> —George W. Bush

★ ★ ★ ★ ★

UNANIMITY

In an act of bitter history-making during the 1820 election, one New Hampshire delegate cast his electoral college vote for an unknown candidate rather than for favorite James Monroe. Why? Because he wanted George Washington to remain the only president in history to be elected unanimously.

★ ★ ★ ★ ★

SACRED SABBATH SERVICES

When Zachary Taylor was inaugurated in May of 1849, he inconvenienced the entire country by refusing to take the Oath of Office on a Sunday. This left the offices of president and vice president vacant for the day, so David Rice Atchison, the president pro tempore of the Senate, had to be sworn in. When asked what he did on his one day as president, Atchison said, "I went to bed. There had been two or three busy nights finishing up the work of the Senate, and I slept most of Sunday."

★ ★ ★ ★ ★

POMP AND HONORARY CIRCUMSTANCE

When thirteenth **President Millard Fillmore was offered an honorary Doctor of Civil Law degree** from Oxford University, he refused. "No man should accept a degree that he cannot read," he said. Eighteen years later, however, Herbert Hoover couldn't have disagreed more. The youngest member of Stanford University's first graduating class, he received more than eighty honorary degrees in his lifetime.

★ ★ ★ ★ ★

WHITE HOUSE WHINERS

Moving into the White House proved quite a drag for twenty-third President Benjamin Harrison. The five-bedroom mansion suddenly seemed small, as he struggled to find space for his daughter's family and several of his wife's relatives who were dying to move in.

After building extra living quarters on 16th Street, the Harrisons found something else to complain about: the food. Apparently French cook Madame Pelouard's pastries just couldn't please the president. According to the New York *Sun*, "the new cook's dishes laid him out," and Harrison let her go in exchange for an African-American chef from Kentucky whose plain-Jane dishes were more pleasing to the Harrison family's picky palate.

If his hollerin' about housing and food weren't enough, Harrison may have suffered from a bit of jealousy as well. His grandchildren, cute little Benjamin and Mary Lodge McKee, were the joys of his life—but they were also a hot topic in the press. Truckloads of toys were delivered to the White House in their name. In fact, the babies received so much attention that Secretary Halford requested that reporters lay off the children and focus on the real political bigwigs. He would have hated, he said, for people to "believe the tales about this child's having more influence than the members of the Cabinet."

> Warren G. Harding once lost all of the White House china gambling on one hand of cards.

★ ★ ★ ★ ★

Celebrity Study Buddies

During his second year at Bowdoin College in Maine, Franklin Pierce attended class with the likes of Nathaniel Hawthorne and Henry Wadsworth Longfellow. Pierce, though, had the worst study habits and the lowest grades of anyone in his class. All first impressions aside, Pierce changed his slacker ways before graduation and ended up placing third in his class.

★ ★ ★ ★ ★

Ready to Run

Despite how rude his ranting may have sounded, James Buchanan may have had good reason to complain about how tired he was of running the country. The nation was becoming increasingly divided over the issue of slavery, and the Whigs were destroyed, giving birth to the Republican Party. Buchanan's excitement for leaving office was so extreme that he actually slipped a note to his successor, Abraham Lincoln, wishing him better luck. "If you are as happy on entering the White House as I on leaving," the note read, "you are a happy man indeed."

Theodore Roosevelt's lifelong interest in zoology began when, at seven years old, he saw a dead seal at a local market.

★ ★ ★ ★ ★

Dirty Draft-Dodgers

When Grover Cleveland was drafted as a young man, he was so scared that he paid someone else to enter the armed forces in his place. During Cleveland's campaign for presidency, his opponent, James Blaine, ridiculed him for his yellow-belly ways, but the public soon discovered Blaine was guilty of the same deception.

Lincoln had a substitute fight for him during the Civil War, but he was no draft dodger. He actually felt strongly that a president should fight alongside his brave countrymen, but his presidential duties precluded his service. J. Summerfield Staples, the son of an army chaplain from Pennsylvania, heard of Lincoln's heartache and volunteered to fight in his place. He survived the war, and today his headstone reads:

> J. Summerfield Staples
> A private of
> Co. C176 Reg. P.V.
> Also a member of the
> 2, Reg. D.C. Vol.
> A substitute for
> Abraham Lincoln
> Died
> Jan. 11, 1888
> Age 43 yrs, 4 mos. & 27 days

★ ★ ★ ★ ★

TAKE ME DRUNK, I'M HOME

After coming down with typhoid fever just days before his vice presidential inauguration, Andrew Johnson found comfort in whiskey. The night before his big day he attended a party with a friend. The next morning a hung over and weak Johnson asked for more whiskey. He was a little tipsy upon arriving at the inauguration ceremony. Obviously feeling ill, he would have preferred to skip the proceedings altogether, but newly elected Lincoln suggested he reconsider. So Johnson showed up and delivered one of the most incoherent, slurred speeches in history.

★ ★ ★ ★ ★

Do the Bush Thing

In 1992, President George H.W. Bush visited Japan for a state dinner with dignitaries including Japanese Prime Minister Kiichi Miyazawa. After turning white as a sheet and nearly sliding out of his seat in pain, he threw up in Miyazawa's lap. Ever since, the Japanese have honored Bush with the word *bushusuru*, which literally means "to do the Bush thing," or to vomit.

★ ★ ★ ★ ★

Indecent Book Proposal

Martin Van Buren was not all that dedicated to treating his wife and family with respect. His home life always took a back seat to his political aspirations. Although he married a young Dutch woman who bore him five sons (it was rumored that the couple spoke Dutch at home), his wife died after twelve years of marriage. Later, when Van Buren penned his autobiography, politics continued to take precedent—he fails to mention his late wife a single time.

DRIVING MISS CRAZY

Ulysses S. Grant was once arrested for driving his horse too fast on the streets of Washington, D.C. The president was fined $20, until the officer at the scene realized he had just pulled over the leader of the country. Grant, however, insisted he comply like any other law-abiding citizen and pay up.

The first president born in the nineteenth century, **Franklin Pierce also had his share of trouble with the law**. He was once charged with running over a woman with his horse, but the charges were dropped in 1853 when a judge decided there was insufficient evidence against him.

ROAD-RAGE REPRIMAND

Woodrow Wilson was a stickler for conscientious driving and refused to accommodate people who even appeared to be traveling faster than he. In fact, he ordered his driver never to exceed twenty miles per hour and believed that anyone going fast enough to pass him was a reckless driver worthy of arrest. He ordered the Secret Service to pull over and question anyone who passed his limousine. However, his agents realized the ridiculous nature of Wilson's request and always returned empty-handed, claiming they simply could not catch the speeders. But the president continued his stubborn road-rage ways, even asking the attorney general to grant him the power to arrest speeding drivers. However, he was denied his request, and the Secret Service persuaded the president that it would be fruitless to go about policing the roadways himself.

★ ★ ★ ★ ★

RAGING RACIST

Richard Nixon was impeached after the government subpoenaed his library of taped conversations. In the process, America gained a whole new insight into the president's sharp personal opinions on an array of topics.

- On Italians: "Difference is … they smell different, look different, act different. … The trouble is, you can't find one that's honest."

- On affirmative action: "With blacks you can usually settle for an incompetent because there are just not enough competent ones."

- On reporters: "I wouldn't give them the sweat off my balls."

- On leadership: "You're never going to make it in politics. You just don't know how to lie."

★ ★ ★ ★ ★

I Cannot Tell A Lie

Telling a tall tale for the sake of political protection, Grover Cleveland once announced he was going on a fishing trip in July 1893. In truth, he was having surgery to remove a strange growth from inside his mouth. Most of his upper-left jaw had to be removed and replaced with an artificial jaw made of vulcanized rubber. He kept the condition under wraps because he feared rumors of his health might darken the country's bleak economic landscape further. The secret was safe with his surgeon, though. The truth didn't surface until twenty-four years later.

★ ★ ★ ★ ★

Million-Dollar Crybaby

Theodore Roosevelt was blind in his left eye. To compensate for the poor physique he inherited in the wake of a sickly childhood, he began working out at the gym and took up boxing lessons. While a student at Harvard University, he lost the boxing championship during an infamous fight with C.S. Hanks. Most people believe Roosevelt was blinded after a punch in a friendly White House boxing match during his term.

★ ★ ★ ★ ★

ROB THE CRADLE OF LOVE

After unexpectedly becoming president when William Henry Harrison died in April of 1841, John Tyler got straight to work (wooing his son's girlfriend, that is). Tyler's son, John Jr., was in love with a young girl named Julia Garner from New York. Julia had probably come to town simply to find herself a husband, and the two met while mingling among society's richest bigwigs. However, before John Jr. could make his move, his father stepped in. While Julia was captivated by the president's power, she refused his proposal of marriage. But when her father was killed in an accident, Julia fainted in despair like a true Southern belle. Tyler came to her rescue and carried her off—the ultimate romantic gesture. She married him June 26, 1844.

★ ★ ★ ★ ★

MEN APART

John Adams and Thomas Jefferson couldn't have had less in common. Adams was a Northerner and a lawyer determined to abolish slavery. Jefferson, on the other hand, was a Virginia man who depended on slavery to maintain his extravagant lifestyle. Regardless, the two men mutually respected each other—until arguments over tactics during the French Revolution and the limits of the president's power tore them apart. Eventually, the two men stopped talking altogether. Publicly expressing his disdain for Adams, Jefferson once said, "He is vain, irritable, and a bad calculator of the force and probable effect of the motives which govern men." Ironically, both men died on the same day: July 4, 1826.

★ ★ ★ ★ ★

RETURN TO SENDER

Quite thrifty when it came to his snail mail, Zachary Taylor refused to cover any postage due on correspondence sent to the White House. After the Postal Service issued its first official stamp (one year before Taylor's nomination), mail was paid for by the recipient rather than the sender. A great war hero from the Mexican War, Taylor was a popular pen pal, but was unwilling to pay the ten-cent charge and, as a result, refused most of his mail. Because of this stingy stance, he didn't receive notification of his nomination as the Whig party's candidate for presidency until several days after the fact.

★ ★ ★ ★ ★

DINNER IS SERVED

Twenty-second **President Grover Cleveland was used to the bachelor life** when he moved into the White House for the first time in 1885. (He served two nonconsecutive terms and returned as the twenty-fourth president in 1893.) He certainly was not accustomed to ornate china,

CLEVELAND

exquisite living quarters, or fine foods. "I must go to dinner," he once wrote in a letter, "but I wish it was to eat a pickled herring, a Swiss cheese, and a chop at Louis' instead of the French stuff I shall find [here]."

★ ★ ★ ★ ★

WHO'S YOUR DADDY

While he may have been a tightwad at the dinner table, Cleveland was even worse when it came to appropriating government money. He once denied desperate farmers in drought-stricken Texas $10,000 worth of seed grain. He also vetoed a bill proposing private pension plans for Civil War veterans who incurred disabilities from somewhere other than the battlefield. Cleveland explained that passing out funds and "running to the financial rescue every time a countryman cried for help would only establish the government as a Daddy to bail everyone out in times of trouble."

★ ★ ★ ★ ★

PRESIDENTIAL POINT-OF-VIEWS

While you may not want to do business with someone who is stubborn and disagreeable, research presented at the American Psychological Association's (APA) annual convention in August 2000

revealed these two character traits are often associated with America's greatest presidents. The report also indicated that "good" presidents were extroverted and assertive, but not straightforward, organized, or vulnerable. In the end, each American president was put in one of eight categories (some fell into more than one group):

- **The Dominators**—Nixon, Andrew Johnson, Lyndon Johnson, Jackson, Polk, Theodore Roosevelt, and Arthur

- **The Introverts**—John Adams, John Quincy Adams, Nixon, Hoover, Coolidge, Buchanan, Wilson, and Benjamin Harrison

- **The Good Guys**—Hayes, Taylor, Eisenhower, Tyler, Fillmore, Cleveland, Ford, and Washington

- **The Innocents**—Taft, Harding, and Grant

- **The Actors**—Reagan, Harding, William Henry Harrison, Clinton, and Pierce

- **The Maintainers**—McKinley, George H.W. Bush, Ford, and Truman

- **The Philosophers**—Garfield, Lincoln, Jefferson, Madison, Carter, and Hayes

- **The Extroverts**—F.D.R., Kennedy, Clinton, Theodore Roosevelt, Reagan, William Henry Harrison, Harding, Jackson, and Lyndon Johnson

Chapter 5

Fads and Fetishes: Presidential Pastimes

CARTER

Fads and Fetishes: Presidential Pastimes

The presidents and their adoring fans get a little out of control when it comes to the things they loved. Whether it's outrageous hobbies, preposterous pets, crazy collections, or the ridiculous gifts they both gave and received, these presidents' personal obsessions were legendary.

DID YOU KNOW

Warren G. Harding had an Airedale dog that sat in his own chair at Cabinet meetings. His dog, Laddie Boy, delivered his newspaper each day. It even had a birthday party, including a cake made of dog biscuits.

★ ★ ★ ★ ★

EARLY ENTREPRENEUR

Jimmy Carter may have been nuts about nuts, but he sometimes took the passion a bit too far. Sure, he became a millionaire when he improved production at the family peanut farm in Georgia, but who would have a giant peanut-shaped balloon at his own inauguration? Well, Carter did … but those who mocked his wacky escapade could learn a thing or two from the country-boy politician with a knack for making a buck. Before his peanut fame, at just nine years old, Carter bought a few bales of cotton for just five cents per pound and stored them until inflation caused the price to more than triple.

★ ★ ★ ★ ★

THE BREAKFAST OF CHAMPIONS

A kid at heart, Lyndon B. Johnson loved Fresca soda so much that he had the fountain drink installed in the White House. With the push of a button, he

Quite curious of psychic phenomena, Abraham Lincoln and his wife held regular séances on the White House grounds.

could have a cold one anytime—even first thing in the morning. Johnson wasn't the only president with wacky mid-morning cravings:

- **Ulysses S. Grant** regularly ate a cucumber soaked in vinegar for breakfast.

- **Calvin Coolidge** loved to have someone rub Vaseline on his head while he ate breakfast in bed each morning.

- **Franklin Delano Roosevelt's** wife, Eleanor, ate three chocolate-covered garlic balls every morning to improve her memory.

DID YOU KNOW? John Quincy Adams owned a pet alligator and pet silkworms.

- **Theodore Roosevelt's** love affair with coffee made Maxwell House a huge success. One cold morning, while visiting Andrew Jackson's home in Nashville in 1912, he inspired their famed motto when after a warm gulp he said, "That coffee tastes good, even to the last drop!"

★ ★ ★ ★ ★

Marijuana Man

George Washington and Benjamin Franklin may not have been potheads, but while in France raising money for the Revolution, Franklin

took over negotiations with the king so Washington could get home to his marijuana plants in Virginia. He was once quoted as saying, "I wouldn't miss the hemp harvest at Mount Vernon for all the tea in China." However, Washington never planned on getting high off his weed. Hemp, or marijuana, was the number one cash crop at the time and was used to make clothes and paper.

★ ★ ★ ★ ★

CARD SHARKS AND LINK LOVERS

During their two-term stay at the White House, Dwight and Mamie Eisenhower were obsessed with playing cards. In fact, they would regularly fly friends in to Washington, D.C., to make sure they had enough gamers for bridge night. Their addiction, however, never matched Old Ike's obsession with hitting the links. During his two-term presidency, he spent an incredible 150 days a year playing golf and even had a putting green built on the White House lawn.

Eisenhower was also quite picky about his help. Years serving as the most powerful man in the nation must have gone to his head, because he eventually demanded that someone help dress him daily. Assistant John Moaney was known to put the president's watch and even his underpants on Eisenhower. Once he left the

fabulous firsts
First president to host Thanksgiving Dinner at the White House: James Polk

White House, Eisenhower was completely unable to take care of himself. He had to learn how to turn on the television and even dial a phone for the first time in years.

★ ★ ★ ★ ★

These Are A Few of My Favorite Things

The oldest man to ever serve as president, Ronald Reagan caused quite a stir when he announced both his guilty pleasures and his medical provisions. When he purchased a hearing aid during his White House reign, sales for the product went up a whopping 40 percent in the

United States. When he joked with the press about his sweet tooth and obsession with the bowl of jelly beans in the Oval Office, sales of jelly beans also skyrocketed (some records say the White House purchased twelve tons of the candy during his term).

★ ★ ★ ★ ★

Less (Clothing) Is More

An avid skinny-dipper, John Quincy Adams was committed to taking nude baths in the Potomac River nearly every morning at dawn (when the weather agreed, of course). Anne Royall, a curious national journalist desperate for an interview, went to the river one morning to try and catch him at one of his most ... vulnerable moments. Refusing to leave without a decent quote, Royall sat on the president's change of clothes until he bashfully agreed to talk to her from the water. Before then, no woman had ever interviewed a president.

> "If you have a job in your department that can't be done by a Democrat, then abolish the job."
> —Andrew Jackson

★ ★ ★ ★ ★

Pardon Me

Most people know that Abraham Lincoln was a man of great mercy—when it came to pardons, he loved to rescue indigents on death row. All it took was an influential letter from an admiring fan (or an influential politician), and he would let a criminal off the hook. Lincoln's lenient ways were tested in 1862, when he was asked to authorize the largest mass hanging in American history.

A group of Sioux Indians had murdered more than eight hundred men, women, and children in a Minnesota settlement in an attempt to take over the town and eat their food (they were literally starving to death). A total of 307 Native Americans had been sentenced to death. Afraid that they had been tried unjustly and therefore would be punished unjustly, Lincoln reviewed all 307 convictions. True to form, he pardoned all but thirty-eight of them. It still qualified as the largest mass hanging in the nation's history, and thousands of spectators showed up to watch the executions.

THE UNLIKELY INVENTOR

Thomas Jefferson was a man of many talents, but few people know that his home, Monticello, is sprinkled with an array of peculiar creations. When historians first toured the building, they found inventions including a homemade copy machine, dumbwaiters, a hideaway bed, a calendar clock, and a rotating closet shelf so that—with the turn of a stick—his hanging clothes could spin on display.

LIFE, LIBERTY, AND THE PURSUIT OF FISH

Herbert Hoover was most content in the woods, hiking through rugged trails and fishing for trout. At a meeting for the Izaak Walton League of America, an organization that works to preserve and protect the nation's woods and wildlife, he once said of his favorite pastime, "Man and boy, the American is a fisherman. That comprehensive list of human rights, the Declaration of Independence,

is firm that all men (and boys) are endowed with certain inalienable rights, including life, liberty, and the pursuit of happiness—which obviously includes the pursuit of fish."

Just before his death, Hoover published a book on the topic called *Fishing for Fun and To Wash Your Soul*, reminding his readers of the joy and peace that comes from life in the outdoors.

In fact, Hoover was such an advocate for outdoor exercise that he had White House physician Admiral Joel T. Boone invent a game called Hoover-Ball to keep him fit. A combination of tennis, volleyball, and medicine ball, the game was given its name by a clever *New York Times* reporter in a 1931 article titled "At the White House at 7 a.m." Early each morning, a group of four to eighteen friends known as the Medicine Ball Cabinet would show up for the Hoover-Ball games on the White House lawn.

★ ★ ★ ★ ★

 For Love of the Game

Herbert Hoover wasn't the only sports fan to grace the White House. **Grace Coolidge, wife of thirtieth President Calvin**

RULES OF HOOVER-BALL

- Teams of 2-4 players play on a 66-by-30-foot court

- Equipment: Six-pound medicine ball and an 8-foot volleyball net

- Scoring is modeled after tennis, and teams play best-of-five or best-of-seven games.

- The ball is served from the back line, and points are scored when a team fails to catch a return, fails to return the ball across the net, or returns the ball out of bounds.

- There is no running with the ball or passing to teammates before throwing the ball back over the net.

- A ball returned from the front half of the court must be returned to the back half of the opponent's court.

- A ball that hits the out-of-bounds line is counted as in.

- A ball that hits the net on its way over is a live ball.

- Women's rules differ. They may serve from the mid-court line, pass once before a return, and return the ball to any area of the opponent's court.

- Good sportsmanship is required. Points in dispute are played over.

Coolidge, was known as "the greatest White House baseball enthusiast of all time." She called the sport "her very life" and would often implore her husband to make sure they were in town for all the big games at Fenway Park. It is rumored that she would curl up in a chair in the sitting room and knit while she listened to radio play by plays of all the games she could not attend.

Grace also used baseball to fuel her other passion—encouraging children with disabilities. A lip-reading teacher at the Clarke School for the Deaf in Massachusetts, she and Red Sox manager Joe Cronin once organized a special day for local deaf children to attend a Boston game. Her love for the game was so intense that her *Boston Globe* obituary on July 9, 1957, was headlined, "Long Active Red Sox Fan."

★ ★ ★ ★ ★

GOD BLESS US EVERYONE

A loyal reader of the works of Charles Dickens, James A. Garfield attended Dickens's lectures every time he visited the United States. In fact, during one visit, Dickens was doing a formal reading of *A Christmas Carol* when an unruly dog in the building barked obnoxiously just as he read the words "Bless his heart: It's Fezziwig again!" Garfield thought the event was so hilarious that every time he met someone who had attended one of Dickens's readings he greeted them with "Bow wow!"

President Zachary Taylor used to ride his horse in the womanly sidesaddle position as he rode into battle. After the glory days, he kept his old warhorse grazing on the White House lawn for years. Little did he know that visitors would pluck hairs from it for souvenirs.

★ ★ ★ ★ ★

LIGHT 'EM UP

A thorough prankster, George H.W. Bush loves his own sense of humor and often cracks himself up. He made a hobby of messing with the stiff politicians who passed through the White House from time to time. Sometimes he greeted Oval Office visitors with a windup bumblebee that would spin around the floor as they entered the room. He was also known to carry around a voice-activated monkey toy that would bop itself on the head whenever someone started talking. His favorite game, though, was something he called "Light 'em Up." He would roll down the windows in his limousine, pick people out in a crowd, and make them smile. He would look at them until they noticed his goofy stare and realized that the president of the United States was looking right at them. When his target's face lit up in joy, Bush would win the game. "Did I get her? Did I light her up?" he would say.

★ ★ ★ ★ ★

SILLY SUPERSTITIONS

Abraham Lincoln's mother, Nancy, passed on a lifetime worth of obsessions and superstitions to her presidential son. H. Donald Winkler, author of *Lincoln's Ladies*, writes that "a bird flying in the window, a horse's breath on a child's head, a dog crossing a hunter's path—all meant bad luck to Nancy Lincoln and her frontier neighbors."

Woodrow Wilson loved golf so much that he would even play in the winter and use black golf balls so he could spot them in the snow.

The Lincoln family also believed that the brightness of the moon played a huge role in daily decision making. One could only make soap or plant certain trees and vegetables when the moon shone brightly. Above all, Nancy insisted that adversity would plague a project started on a Friday. Abe would spend the rest of his life a bit confused by all the suspicions his mother had taught him at such a young, influential age.

But Lincoln was not the only president to be distracted by superstitions. Dwight Eisenhower carried three coins with him at all times for good

EISENHOWER

luck—a silver dollar, a five-guinea gold piece, and a French franc. Franklin Roosevelt would never light three cigarettes off of the same match, and he hated the number thirteen. He refused to sit at a table set for thirteen guests.

★ ★ ★ ★ ★

 JESUS IS MY HOMEBOY

Touting one's religious affiliation has long been a fad among politicians. Theodore Roosevelt announced some of his most passionate stances as a Christian. At the same time, he strongly opposed the engraving of "In God We Trust" on the nation's new $20 gold coin in 1907. He felt it was blasphemous to put God's name on money so often used to buy "worldly" things, and he pressed for the motto to be removed. Sinful spending aside, the public disagreed with Roosevelt and the motto remains.

Thomas Jefferson was also not afraid to flaunt his fascination with all things religious. It has been argued that his writings communicate a confusing conundrum of beliefs that bounce among Deism, Episcopalianism, and Unitarianism. Jefferson was never an official member of a congregation or denomination, and in some of his works he even rejected the divinity of Jesus Christ.

> **fabulous firsts**
> First president to own a radio: Warren G. Harding

According to a report by the Public Broadcasting Service, "Jefferson was convinced that the authentic words of Jesus written in the New Testament had been contaminated. Early Christians, overly eager to make their religion appealing to the pagans, had obscured the words of Jesus with the philosophy of ancient Greeks and the teachings of Plato."

Jefferson wrote several books based on what he believed to be the true message of Jesus in Christian texts. In 1820 he completed *The Life and Morals of Jesus of Nazareth Extracted Textually from the Gospels in Greek, Latin, French, and English*. In the book, printed after his death and typically referred to as the "Jefferson Bible," Jefferson translated the New Testament in four different languages, omitting any words he thought were "inauthentic." His critics, however, argue that all he did was rearrange passages that either sounded supernatural or simply rubbed him the wrong way.

> "Whenever I hear anyone arguing for slavery, I feel a strong impulse to see it tried on him personally."
> —Abraham Lincoln

Finally, **William McKinley also referenced God when making political decisions.** In 1899, when trying to decide whether to annex the Philippines, he told a group of Methodist clergymen that God told him to go ahead with the deal. Apparently, he had prayed about the issue while pacing around the White House and God finally told him just to consider the islands "a gift from heaven."

★ ★ ★ ★ ★

FURNITURE FASHION POLICE

Chester Arthur may not have planned on taking up the hobby of decorating the White House when he was inaugurated in 1881, but when he first swung open the doors to the famed mansion, he was so appalled at the mismatched furniture that he ordered every piece removed. After a whopping twenty-four wagonloads took the furniture to auction, Arthur had the entire White House remodeled in late Victorian style. When William McKinley moved into the White House in 1897, his wife, Ida, was similarly disgusted with one particular color—yellow. She hated the color so much she forbade its use on the grounds. She even had the gardeners pull every yellow flower out of the garden.

★ ★ ★ ★ ★

PRESIDENTIAL PETS

When it comes to presidential pets, the nation's greatest leaders had some of the most interesting pets to ever grace the country. Check

out the following fun facts on the coolest animals to ever lift a leg on the White House lawn:

- **Lyndon B. Johnson** had two pet beagles named Him and Her. Him's paw prints are actually imprinted in the sidewalk leading up to the White House pressroom. Later, J. Edgar Hoover gave Johnson a third beagle named Edgar.

- **Jimmy Carter** had a dog named Grits.

- **George Washington** had six white horses. He had their teeth brushed every morning.

- **William Henry Harrison** had a pet goat named His Whiskers.

A sucker for weird morning rituals, Thomas Jefferson claims to have soaked his feet in cold bath water every day for sixty years. He said it was what led to his unusually long lifespan of eighty-three years.

- **Martin Van Buren** was given two tiger cubs by the Sultan of Oman in 1837, but Congress decided they were a gift to the American people—not just the president—and the animals went to the zoo.

- **William McKinley's** pet parrot could whistle "Yankee Doodle."

- **Woodrow Wilson** kept a flock of sheep on the White House lawn. He often used their wool to raise money for the Red Cross during World War I. One of the sheep, named Old Ike, was rumored to chew tobacco.

- **Calvin Coolidge** had a number of dogs and cats, as well as a donkey named Ebenezer, a raccoon named Rebecca, and a goose that was once cast in a Broadway play.

- At the height of the Cold War, Russian Premiere Khrushchev sent **John F. Kennedy's daughter, Caroline**, a dog named Pushinka.

It was the puppy of the first dog in space, Strelka. Before Kennedy allowed his daughter to take the pooch, he had the army x-ray it for bugging devices.

• Explorers Lewis and Clark gave **Thomas Jefferson** two grizzly bear cubs. He was so fascinated by them that he had a cage built on the White House lawn so all visitors could marvel at the beasts from the West.

• **George H. W. Bush's** wife, Barbara, had a spaniel named Millie that was once referred to as "the ugliest dog in the capital." Ignoring the comment, the First Lady went on to write the bestselling *Millie's Book*, a look at life in the White House through her dog's eyes.

> **fabulous firsts**
>
> First president to use loudspeakers at his inauguration: Warren G. Harding

Less than twenty miles from the White House, The Presidential Pet Museum in Lothian, Maryland, is a mecca for presidential-pet fanatics. Founded in 1999 as a means to "preserve information, artifacts, and items" related to all the animals who have ever scratched or sniffed their way around the presidential mansion, the museum displays more than 1,500 "items of interest," including a portrait of Reagan's Bouvier des Flandres and photos of George Washington's pony. A little too highbrow for walk-ins, the museum can be toured only by appointment.

★ ★ ★ ★ ★

PRESENTS FOR THE PRESIDENTS

Presidents have had both friends and enemies among the American public. Many of them make a hobby out of collecting cheesy, handmade creations from their adoring fans. Some of the most unsightly gifts have been put on display across the country.

An exhibition in the Circular Gallery of the National Archives put some of these thoughtful, yet sometimes hideous, collections on display in March 1996. And while the gifts are unusual (for lack of a better word), museum officials' overzealous descriptions were even worse. "Although most of the artists represented are not well known, their works are no less striking," a commemoration on a government website reads. "Often expertly crafted, these gifts are heartfelt expressions of admiration and affection for the president." You be the judge.

★ ★ ★ ★ ★

RIDE 'EM COWBOY

This wooden image of a cowboy lassoing Adolf Hitler was given to Franklin D. Roosevelt by Secretary of Commerce Jesse Jones during the first few months of World War II.

Image provided by White House Historical Association

★ ★ ★ ★ ★

These Boots Were Made For Walking

Image provided by White House Historical Association

These hand-painted, steel-toe shoes were customized for President Eisenhower. Complete with symbols of the U.S. Capitol, the Great Seal of the United States, and sunflowers from his home state of Kansas, they're some patriotic footwear.

★ ★ ★ ★ ★

Caricatures Gone Wrong

Image provided by White House Historical Association

When Lyndon B. Johnson was recovering from gallbladder surgery in the middle of his six-year term, Texan Gene Zesch thought he would brighten the president's day with a painted wooden figure representing his great progress. Although Johnson had certainly made political strides, signing more than two hundred bills into law during his term, he was probably a little alarmed by the not-so-flattering depiction of his persona.

Image provided by White House Historical Association

Like a laughable marionette, this **Richard Nixon** look-alike doll was given to the president as a symbol of America's victory in World War II.

Finally, **Gerald Ford** received this painted Pennsylvania river stone from Michael Manning of Pennsylvania in 1976. At a whopping seventy pounds, the rendering makes the president look quite round.

Image provided by White House Historical Association

★ ★ ★ ★ ★

OPERATION CHESS

During Operation Desert Storm in the early 1990s, E. Howard Kellogg's nephew was held hostage in Iraq. Kellogg found comfort in recreating the battlefield at home with a handmade chess set. After America's victory and his nephew's safe return, Kellogg mailed the game set to President George H.W. Bush for safekeeping.

Image provided by White House Historical Association

114

HALF-ASSED

When Harry S. Truman enacted his Fair Deal domestic program, calling for increased funding for education, a tax cut, an end to discrimination, and new economic support for farmers, Secretary of Agriculture Charles F.

Image provided by White House Historical Association

Brannon was so thrilled that he sent Truman this giant papier mâché donkey for a job well done.

"Things are more like they are now than they ever were before."
—Dwight Eisenhower

Chapter 6

Fast Times and First Ladies: Women Behind the White House

MADISON

Fast Times and First Ladies: Women Behind the White House

Over the past 250 years, the first ladies have sported a wide range of perky (and parched) personalities. Among all their quirky habits and hobbies, they left a long list of legacies. Lou Henry Hoover helped found the Girl Scouts of America. Eleanor Roosevelt tried to take up shooting but couldn't hit a target with her gun if she wanted to. Julia Dent Grant was cross-eyed. Some were hot-tempered, antisocial, and overzealous. Others were bookworms, some were accused of adultery, and many more were groundbreaking fashionistas. Regardless of their differences, each first lady left a lasting impact as she stood by her husband during his years in office.

> During his first three years as president, Hoover and his wife dined alone only on their wedding anniversary.

★ ★ ★ ★ ★

I'M SORRY, MRS. JACKSON

When Rachel Donelson and Andrew Jackson married in 1791, they had no idea that Rachel's former husband, Lewis

> "Mrs. Monroe hath added a daughter to our society who, tho' noisy, contributes greatly to its amusement."
> —James Monroe

Robards, had never actually filed their divorce papers. Though it was an honest mix-up, a cloud of rumored adultery hung over Rachel's head.

Jackson stood by Rachel's reputation and was extremely sensitive to accusations anyone made regarding the legal mistake. His reactions often resulted in violent outbursts. In 1806, Charles Dickinson made the mistake of muttering something crude, which resulted in a heated exchange between the two men. During the subsequent argument, Dickinson shot Jackson in the chest, just a few inches from his heart. But Jackson was too enraged to collapse in pain. Instead, he shot and killed Dickinson and then walked away. The bullet lodged so close to Jackson's vital organs that doctors opted not to operate, so he bore the consequence of his famous duel for the rest of his life.

Jackson also threatened to cut off the ears of a man who accused him of infidelity, and he later challenged Tennessee Governor John

Sevier to a duel after *his* comments about Mrs. Jackson. After offering a long apology, Sevier was pardoned, and Jackson withdrew his plans for revenge. Ultimately, Rachel died before Jackson ever took office, but he defended her purity and innocence on her tombstone in the garden at The Hermitage just outside

According to some records, John Tyler was so poor that just five years after leaving office, he was unable to pay a bill for $1.25.

Nashville, Tennessee. Her epitaph reads, "A being so gentle and so virtuous slander might wound, but could not dishonor."

★ ★ ★ ★ ★

Good Golly, Mrs. Dolley

Political socialites were shocked when shy, taciturn James Madison announced his engagement to the vibrant and animated political party girl Dolley Payne Todd, who had occasionally hosted soirees for the Jefferson administration. Raised in Quaker-influenced

Philadelphia, Dolley grew up under strict discipline. But once Philadelphia became the capital city and cute, young politicians came to town, she let down her dark curls and soaked up the attention. By the time she married Madison, then a U.S. Representative, she had become a local trendsetter and quite the entertainer. Often criticized for gambling, wearing excessive makeup, and using tobacco, Dolley seemed like an unlikely match for Madison, but she went on to become one of the most popular First Ladies to grace the White House. Her fame and fortune outlived her husband's, and she continued to enjoy the city's social life long after his term was over.

★ ★ ★ ★ ★

Be Our Guest

After Dolley Madison's exciting escapades, American gossip queens were not so pleased with shy newcomer Elizabeth Monroe. Regardless of the sophistication she acquired while living abroad in Great Britain and France, where she was known as "*la belle Americaine,*" Elizabeth immediately abandoned Dolley's traditions of holding regular open houses and entertaining diplomats' wives at lavish dinner parties. When she did try out a new social schedule, the press balked at the guests present at the formal affairs. One journalist for *Munsey's Magazine* wrote, "The secretaries, senators ... farmers, merchants, parsons, priests, lawyers, judges, auctioneers, and

> "Forget that I'm president of the United States. I'm Warren Harding, playing poker with friends, and I'm going to beat the hell out of them."
> —Warren G. Harding

nothingarians—all with their wives and some of their gawky offspring—crowd to the president's house every Wednesday evening; some in shoes, most in boots, and many in spurs; some snuffing, others chewing, and many longing for their cigars and whiskey punch left at home; some with powdered heads, some frizzled and oiled; some whose heads a comb has never touched, half hid by dirty collars."

★ ★ ★ ★ ★

Every Party Has A Pooper

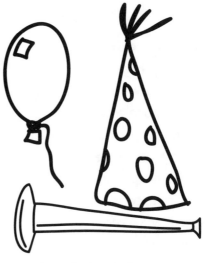

The first woman to ever be called "First Lady of the Land," Rutherford B. Hayes's wife, Lucy, took her reformed White House duties to the extreme. Likely as a direct result of her family's strict religious beliefs, she banned smoking and card playing from government grounds during her husband's term. She was nicknamed Lemonade Lucy by her more worldly cohorts angered by her passionate stance against alcohol.

James K. Polk's administration was also a dud when it came to partying. His wife, Sarah, banned dancing at the White House (she didn't even dance at the Inaugural Ball) and refused to attend the theater or local horse races. To make matters worse, Polk considered it a waste of money to provide refreshments to his (probably bored) guests. With so many rules to remember, it is no wonder he died of exhaustion just after his term ended.

★ ★ ★ ★ ★

READY, AIM, MISFIRE

When it came to protecting Franklin Roosevelt's wife, Eleanor, from any harm, he simply was not able to overcome her stubborn independence. Eleanor refused to be escorted by Secret Service agents, so government officials gave her lessons on how to use a personal handgun.

But after a trip with her to the FBI firing range, then-FBI Chief J. Edgar Hoover had his doubts. "Mr. President," he said, "if there is one person in the U.S. who should not carry a gun, it's your wife. She cannot hit a barn door."

★ ★ ★ ★ ★

TOMBOY TURNED GIRL SCOUT

"The independent girl is truly of quite modern origin, and usually is a most bewitching little piece of humanity," wrote fifteen-year-old Lou Henry. Later the eccentric wife of outdoorsman President Herbert Hoover, Lou was a revolutionary during a time when most women were confined to the home. Known for her history of fishing and camping with her father, Lou was recruited by Juliette Low to serve as a founding member of the Girl Scouts. She is credited with initiating the Girl Scout cookie sale during her second term as president of the organization.

Lou's involvement in the Girl Scouts was a reflection of her inner tomboy. She loved camping in the Sierra Mountains, studied at the London School of Mines, and became the first woman in the United States to earn a degree in geology. The day after her wedding, in February 1899, she left on a series of world travels that would eventually take her to China, Belgium, France, Russia, New Zealand, Australia, Burma, and Egypt.

During Hoover's term as president, the couple built Camp Rapidan, a rustic fishing resort in Virginia's Shenandoah Mountains. There, they threw horseshoes with Charles Lindbergh and sat on a log brainstorming with other world leaders about upcoming issues and conferences. "The joyous rush of the brook, the contemplation of the eternal flow of the stream, the stretch of forest and mountain all reduce our egotism, smooth our troubles, and shame our wickedness," Lou wrote.

The only president never to be married, James Buchanan had his niece act as first lady.

★ ★ ★ ★ ★

Anything You Can Do I Can Do Better

All of the first ladies who have passed through the White House differ in talents and tastes. In 1980, editors at *Good Housekeeping* magazine decided to rank the presidential hostesses based on their role as hostess, campaigner, leader in causes, feminist, and traditionalist. The editors also considered their interest in politics, improvements made to the White House, influence on the president, helpfulness to the president, outspokenness, charisma, and inspiration to other women.

"I think the American public wants a solemn ass as president, and I think I'll go along with them."—Calvin Coolidge

SUBSIDIZING SON

Tad Lincoln, son of Abraham and Mary Todd, was born with a cleft palate that caused him to have a frustrating lisp and a hard time eating. However, Tad put his sob story aside and spent much of his boyhood as an advocate for the Sanitary Commission—a Civil War organization similar to today's Red Cross or Salvation Army. At just eleven years old, he was one of their most eager fundraisers, and his moneymaking schemes were both elaborate and conniving.

The assessment wasn't exactly scientific, but the results were as follows:

1. Lady Bird Johnson

2. Eleanor Roosevelt

3. Rosalynn Carter

4. Lou Hoover

5. Jackie Kennedy

6. Betty Ford

7. Helen Taft

8. Pat Nixon

9. Bess Truman

10. Florence Harding

11. Edith Roosevelt

John Tyler was playing marbles when he learned he was to become president.

12. Edith Wilson

13. Grace Coolidge

14. Mamie Eisenhower

15. Ellen Wilson

MUSICAL INTERLUDE

President John Tyler's wife, Julia, was the first person to initiate the tradition of playing "Hail to the Chief" whenever the president appeared in public. The piece was originally written for the stage version of *The Lady of the Lake*, a poem by Sir Walter Scott. The tune was retitled "Wreaths for the Chieftain" and given new lyrics for the late George Washington's 1815 birthday celebration in Boston. It was first performed by the Marine Band on July 4, 1828, at a ceremony attended by President John Quincy Adams. Julia Tyler made the band's performance a regular affair, and Sarah Polk (of the next administration) followed her lead. The song has been associated with the commander in chief's presence ever since.

JOKING WITH THE JESUS FREAK

When James K. Polk asked Andrew Jackson for dating advice in 1823, Jackson replied that he should marry "the one who will never give you no trouble." With that, Polk pursued Sarah

Childress, the daughter of a well-to-do merchant from Murfreesboro, Tennessee. He may have thought she was tame at first, but Sarah could be anything but reserved. During her husband's 1844 campaign, she was taunted by a supporter of opponent Henry Clay who said that Mrs. Clay would make a better first lady because she made a dang tasty batch of butter and was a very "economical housekeeper." With a bitter look, Sarah replied that she could run the family budget so well that she would never *have* to make her own butter.

From time to time, however, Sarah was quite prudish and was often teased for her devout religious commitments. She was famous for insisting on taking to church any of Polk's associates who visited the White House on a Sunday. Aware of her tradition, one particular politician decided to play a joke on her when she told him there was a new preacher in the pulpit that day. "I would like to go with you, Madam, for I have played cards with him many a time!" Of course he was kidding, aware that Sarah disapproved of the sinful practice of card playing and dancing.

When Abigail Powers Fillmore saw the scarcity of books in the White House, she immediately had her husband ask Congress to appropriate money for a new presidential library on the second floor of the mansion. Many of the books she acquired remain there today.

Another night, over dinner at the White House, a friend from South Carolina said, "Madam, I have long wished to see the lady upon whom the Bible pronounces a woe!" Shocked at the apparent insult, everyone at the table waited for his explanation. "Does not the Bible say, 'Woe unto you when all men shall speak well of you?'" Relieved that the comment was actually a compliment, Sarah and her guests burst into laughter.

★ ★ ★ ★ ★

MISERY LOVES COMPANY

Although Martha Washington burned most of the letters exchanged between George, herself, and their beloved family and friends after his death, a few surviving pieces of correspondence reveal that she was miserable in her role as first lady. "I think I am more like a state prisoner than anything else, there is certain bounds set for me which I must not depart from," she once wrote. However, Martha did her best to remain cheerful both in private and public, for "the greater part of our happiness or misery," she wrote, "depends upon our dispositions, not upon our circumstances."

★ ★ ★ ★ ★

DEAR JOHN

During his lengthy relationship with Ann Rutledge, Abraham Lincoln had to put up quite a fight to win her from previous suitor John McNeil, who had once wooed Ann while Lincoln was running for the

legislature. Although considered quite a catch in their New Salem hometown, McNeil dropped a bomb on Rutledge after their engagement—he had a double life. His real name was McNamar, and he was going to New York to bring his underprivileged family back to Illinois to enjoy the fortune he had worked so hard to acquire. He had allegedly changed his name for fear that they would find and move in with him before he had time to "accumulate any property." Many people believed Ann was a fool for believing such a tale and ostracized her for being ditched by the town's most eligible bachelor.

After being romanced by Lincoln, Ann was in better spirits and wrote her former fiancé, whom she had not heard from in a year, that she would soon marry another. He sent no reply, but months later Ann received a letter in which McNamar expressed his excitement to finally be home and married to her. Either he had not received her Dear John letter, or he wanted to guilt her back into his arms. With the help of girlfriends at home, Ann stood her ground and planned to tell him about her relationship with Lincoln and dump him for good as soon as he returned. Unfortunately, she fell ill with what the local doctor called "brain fever" and died before she had the chance.

★ ★ ★ ★ ★

The Doghouse Blues

Lincoln may have suffered a bout of depression after his first love died in her early twenties, but he soon married Mary Todd, who would take him to new levels of frustration. A hotheaded woman with a flaring temper, she threw tantrums that would earn their home the nickname "suburb of Hades." She chased Abe out of the house with broomsticks, threw books across the room, and tossed a servant boy's suitcase out of a second-floor window. When political friend Jesse K. Dubois walked Lincoln home after work one day, Mary met them at the door and screamed, "You brought the wrong kind of meat! I can't use this!" and slapped him in the face. Needless to say, Abe frequently slept on the couch in his office.

INQUIRING PHOTOGRAPHERS WANT TO KNOW

Jacqueline Lee Bouvier, future wife of President John F. Kennedy, once won first place in a *Vogue* magazine Prix de Paris contest, in which she submitted a composition and was quizzed in an interview with the publication's editors. However, instead of accepting their offer to work for the magazine, she accepted a job at the *Washington Times Herald*, where she put together the "Inquiring Photographer" column for $42.50 per week.

Jackie's articles were anything but hard news—she would feature a local person's photograph next to their answer to simple questions such as "Have you done your

Christmas shopping?" or "Do women marry because they are too lazy to go to work?" On November 7, 1952, her column featured Richard Nixon's six-year-old daughter, who commented on whether her father was fit to take over the presidency. Her quote read, "He's always away. If he's famous, why can't he stay home?"

★ ★ ★ ★ ★

SINGING SORORITY GIRL

Long before she married Calvin Coolidge in 1905, Grace Anna Goodhue founded a chapter of the Phi Beta Phi women's fraternity at the University of Vermont. A "sister" through and through, she maintained close ties with the chapter even after she moved to the White House in 1923. In April 1924, 1,300 fraternity members assembled in the East Room of the White House to present a portrait of Grace with her collie to the White House Collection. If the crowded celebration weren't enough, the girls formed a semicircle around the room and sang the Phi Beta Phi anthem to their beloved alumna.

The candy bar Baby Ruth was named after Grover Cleveland's daughter, Ruth.

★ ★ ★ ★ ★

SNEAKIN' OUT

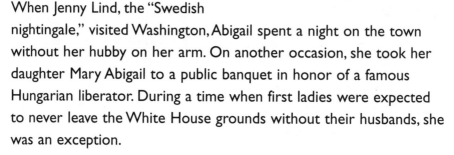

While this ex-schoolteacher never really spoke up about women's rights, when Abigail Powers Fillmore's husband became president, she occasionally broke the mold and rebelled against the proscribed roles of a wealthy politician's wife. When Jenny Lind, the "Swedish nightingale," visited Washington, Abigail spent a night on the town without her hubby on her arm. On another occasion, she took her daughter Mary Abigail to a public banquet in honor of a famous Hungarian liberator. During a time when first ladies were expected to never leave the White House grounds without their husbands, she was an exception.

★ ★ ★ ★ ★

OPPOSITES ATTRACT

Franklin and Jane Pierce were an unlikely pair from the beginning. He was an outgoing Democrat who loved mingling with loud, boisterous politicians. Her family members were Whigs, she was shy and socially awkward, and she was often annoyed by her husband's devotion to politics. Although they could appreciate his ambition, Jane's relatives warned her that her husband-to-be was rumored to drink a little too much.

The story of how the couple met, however, is quite romantic. While studying in the Bowdoin College library, Jane saw dark clouds accumulating outside the window and rushed out the door so she could make it home before the storm broke. As she ran, the rain burst from the sky and a clap of thunder sent her huddling under an old oak tree. Franklin Pierce, another student at Bowdoin, ran to her rescue, explaining that she was likely to get struck by lightning when holding a tree so tightly. He took her in his arms and escorted her home—the rest is history.

★ ★ ★ ★ ★

THOSE LYIN' EYES

Julia Dent Grant was cross-eyed and often toyed with the idea of having corrective surgery while her husband was president. However, as she was verifying the appointment, her husband talked her out of it, saying, "I don't want you to have your eyes fooled with. ... They look just as they did the very first time I ever saw them—the same eyes I looked into when I fell in love with you." Julia had only scheduled the surgery because she thought it would please her husband, so she canceled the appointment and was cross-eyed until the day she died in December 1902.

★ ★ ★ ★ ★

ARSENIC EXFOLIANT

Frances Cleveland never gave advertisers permission to use her name and photograph in their print advertisements for medicine and soap. However, one ascribed Frances's attractiveness to her use of arsenic as a facial cleanser. "Mrs. Cleveland's Remarkable and Beautiful Complexion," it read. "The secret of her beautiful complexion … is simply the use of arsenic, which can safely be taken and which can be procured from the New York doctor whose name is signed to this advertisement." Frances received a large stack of letters from Americans who could not believe she would sell her likeness to promote such a product, and the event prompted the National Women's Temperance Convention to prohibit "the immoral exhibition of the faces and forms of noted women."

★ ★ ★ ★ ★

THE WRITE STUFF

While previous presidential wives may have been a little half-hearted when it came to keeping up with pen pals, Eleanor Roosevelt seriously considered responding to all of the 300,000 letters she received in 1933. She threw away the hate mail, passed the rest on to the appropriate departments, and personally replied to the more important letters.

Amid the gaggle of fans, there was sure to be a nutcase or two. One woman wrote asking Eleanor to help her adopt a baby. A second letter said that once she got the baby, she would need a cow

… and then an icebox in which to put the milk. Other women wrote to complain about hemorrhoids, hernias, and "female troubles." No matter how off-color the requests, Eleanor managed to reply with grace and love.

As if replying to ridiculous fan mail didn't cramp her hand enough, Eleanor took up journalism in the 1920s and 1930s. She was a monthly columnist for *Woman's Home Companion*, writing on a variety of topics from education to gardening and old age to traditional morals. In 1941, she committed to another monthly column called "If You Ask Me" in *Ladies' Home Journal* (the column later moved to *McCall's*). Each month, she gave inquisitive readers her honest opinions and anecdotes about life as the first lady.

★ ★ ★ ★ ★

The President's Wives Pass Away

Unfortunately for their husbands, a few first ladies died in the midst of their rise to political immorality.

- **Martha Wayles Skelton Jefferson**—The wife of third President Thomas Jefferson, Martha and four of Jefferson's six children died nineteen years before he became president. He kept his promise to never remarry and had socialite Dolley Payne, who would later marry James Madison, serve as the "unofficial hostess" of White House social affairs.

- **Letitia Christian Tyler**—The wife of tenth President John Tyler, Letitia moved into the White House in 1841 paralyzed from a stroke. She only appeared in public once while her husband was president—at her daughter Elizabeth's wedding. She and Tyler had eight children, and within a few months of Elizabeth's wedding, she had a second stroke and died.

- **Ellen Lewis Herndon Arthur**—The wife of twenty-first President Chester Arthur, Ellen died just a few months before her husband moved into the White House. Because the couple's only child was just ten years old at the time, Arthur appointed his sister to act as hostess. To honor his wife's memory, he was known to put a vase of fresh flowers under Ellen's portrait every day.

- **Caroline Scott Harrison**—The wife of twenty-third President Benjamin Harrison, Caroline was bedridden by a bout of tuberculosis while serving as first lady. She died less than one month before her husband lost his bid for reelection in 1893.

- **Ellen Axson Wilson**—The wife of twenty-eighth President Woodrow Wilson, Ellen suffered from a kidney disorder called Bright's disease and died at the White House during her husband's first term. Until Wilson remarried in 1915, Ellen's daughter, Margaret, handled all the womanly duties at the executive mansion.

- **Rachel Donelson Jackson**—The wife of seventeenth President Andrew Jackson, Rachel died of a heart attack not long after her husband was elected president. Because the Jacksons had no children, Rachel's niece Emily took over as chief entertainer

Chapter 7

Hot and Not: Political Highs and Lows

KENNEDY

Hot and Not:
Political Highs and Lows

Not all of the United States' presidents posed as nude models for their college classmates in their younger days, but many of them had their own ways of adapting to (or rebelling against) the latest fashions of their time. Some had unusual biological challenges in terms of their appearance (such as Kennedy's stubby leg and Carter's missing testicle), while others effortlessly captivated the ladies. Love them or hate them, here is the skinny on the high-maintenance studs and their charming ways.

> ## DID YOU KNOW
> James Madison was the shortest and slightest president at 5 feet, 4 inches and only one hundred pounds.

★ ★ ★ ★ ★

RATS TAIL REBELLION

Andrew Johnson was the only president to sew his own clothes.

Not a fan of the high-society fashions of the late 1700s, George Washington refused to wear a powdered wig like the rest of the aristocrats of his time. As a compromise, he instead rubbed white powder through his reddish brown hair and tied it in a short braid down his back.

Thomas Jefferson wasn't a fan of the elaborate British fashion trends either. To him, the Revolution had done away with England's tyranny and anything that suggested it. He just wanted to be another "voting member of the public" and couldn't wait to ditch the ridiculous attire and start acting like an average Joe.

★ ★ ★ ★ ★

REAGAN'S FULL MONTY

While in college in 1940, Ronald Reagan was voted "Most Nearly Perfect Male Figure" by his classmates at the University of California. His prize? The opportunity to pose nude for university art students learning how to sculpt the human body.

fabulous firsts
First president sworn in wearing long trousers: John Quincy Adams

MODEL ATHLETE

Gerald Ford was a stud long before he took office and long after, some would say. A member of the University of Michigan football team from 1931-1934, he was offered professional tryouts with the Green Bay Packers and the Chicago Bears. But instead he went on to coach at Yale while studying law. In 1939, he and his girlfriend tried their hand at modeling and were pictured in a *Look* magazine article about the lives of the country's most beautiful people. Three years later, he got his next big break on the cover of *Cosmopolitan*.

But was Ford all brawn and no brains? It could seem that way. His history in front of the camera may have made him a little hard to take seriously, and his countless clumsy conundrums made his reputation even worse. Whether he was accidentally locking himself out of the White House or tumbling down the steps of Air Force One, Ford couldn't deny being a klutz. He quickly became the joke of news reports and late-night comedy skits around the world.

DID YOU KNOW?
Abraham Lincoln was the tallest president at 6 feet, 4 inches.

★ ★ ★ ★ ★

Man In Uniform

In December 2004, George W. Bush became the first U.S. president to wear a uniform when he sported a traditional military jacket while addressing the troops in Marine Corps base Camp Pendleton. Even former Presidents Eisenhower and Grant never donned military garb when they ceased to be generals and switched to civilian clothes (as would be expected from Bush). Traditionally, only dictatorial national leaders wear uniforms.

Often depicted wearing a tall black stovepipe hat, sixteenth President Abraham Lincoln was rumored to carry letters, bills, and notes in his hat.

★ ★ ★ ★ ★

There Was A Crooked Man...

President John F. Kennedy, a Democrat from Brookline, Massachusetts, had one leg significantly longer than the other. To correct his crooked stance, he had to wear corrective shoes to make up the 3/4-inch difference.

KENNEDY

SMOKIN' SHOULDERS

Woodrow Wilson once described Franklin Delano Roosevelt as "the handsomest young giant I have ever seen." The quote was a friendly tease. Although FDR was 6 feet, 2 inches tall and weighed 190 pounds, he lost the use of his legs to polio. Soon after he was confined to a wheelchair, he buffed up his upper body to build some impressive muscle. "Maybe my legs aren't so good, but look at these shoulders! Jack Dempsey would be green with envy," he once said.

The president was known to make light of his disability. When Madame Chiang Kai-shek visited the White House during his term, she politely asked him not to bother with standing out of respect as she rose to leave the room. "My dear child," he laughed, "I couldn't stand up if I had to!"

BATHTUB BLUES

Historically remembered as the tubbiest commander in chief to hold office, William H. Taft tipped the scales at more than three hundred pounds. Most accounts of his presidency are quick to point out his troubles fitting

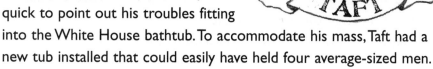

into the White House bathtub. To accommodate his mass, Taft had a new tub installed that could easily have held four average-sized men.

★ ★ ★ ★ ★

A Face for Radio

Although not a big fan of his own appearance, Woodrow Wilson was a good sport about his awkward reflection. He once made up a limerick about himself that read:

> For beauty I am not a star
> There are others more handsome by far
> But my face I don't mind it
> For I am behind it
> It's the people in front that I jar.

Abraham Lincoln may have had charm, wit and wisdom, but he was shy about his looks and was often lighthearted about his appearance. During a debate in 1858, Stephen Douglas called him two-faced. Lincoln replied, "If I had another face, do you think I would wear this one?" And finally, Lyndon B. Johnson was so disgusted with the way he looked in his official presidential portrait that he would not allow it to hang anywhere in the White House. He said the painting was "the ugliest thing I ever saw."

Franklin Delano Roosevelt's mother forced him to wear dresses until he was five years old.

DID YOU KNOW
McKinley liked to wear a white vest and a lucky red carnation in his buttonhole.

★ ★ ★ ★ ★

CLOTHES HORSE

Charming, sweet-talking Chester Arthur never would have become president if his predecessor, James A. Garfield, hadn't died in office. Arthur was a heck of a dresser and was rumored to have owned as many as eighty pairs of pants. With a love for all things lavish, he spent much of his time dressed to the nines and riding in his laughably extravagant carriage—complete with gold lace curtains and the Arthur family coat of arms emblazoned on the side.

Chester Arthur, who changed clothes often, was nicknamed "Elegant Arthur."

★ ★ ★ ★ ★

HAIR TODAY, GONE TOMORROW

CNN Washington Bureau writer Bruce Morton wasn't kidding when he reported on the effectiveness of Former Vice President Al Gore's "salt-and-pepper" speckled beard in 2002. In his online article, Morton suggested that Gore follow the lead of past presidents and give his face a clean shave. No president has sported

DID YOU KNOW

Washington wore size 13 shoes, was 6 feet, 2 inches tall, and weighed about 175 pounds (until he put on about twenty-five more pounds later in life).

facial hair in the last century, he wrote, and only five presidents had a beard or mustache before then. Abraham Lincoln may have struck gold when he followed the advice of an

fabulous firsts
First president to set up a Christmas tree in the White House: Franklin Pierce

eleven-year-old girl who told him he should grow out his whiskers for the 1860 election—but he was a rare exception. Some speculate that Thomas Dewey was the last presidential candidate with facial hair to run for office. He and his dashing mustache just couldn't seem to swing the votes his way in 1944 or 1948. After his two miserable losses, candidates took

Jimmy Carter had only one testicle.

note of Dewey's grubby, hobo-like looks, and nothing but a five o'clock shadow has been sported since.

★ ★ ★ ★ ★

HARRISON LETS HIMSELF GO

After his term ended in 1893, Benjamin Harrison lost his edge as a bachelor. He enjoyed the lazy days of early retirement and took up the hobby of ... doing nothing. He moved home to Indianapolis and took a long, lethargic break from anything that required too much brain power. Some say he took an entire day to unpack one box of china, then crawled back into bed. His one commitment, however, was turning down offers for jobs as a lawyer or the president of a bank. Instead, he charged *Ladies' Home Journal* $5,000 for a handful of freelance articles.

DID YOU KNOW

Besides being known for his bulging shoulder muscles, FDR was also quite the trendsetter when it came to clothes that were easy for his personal assistants to dress him in. Because putting on a heavy overcoat was so difficult, he became known for his trademark navy cape, which kept him warm during the winter.

While most would assume Harrison's break from the social scene (and the working world) would serve as a turnoff to most women, Harrison's charm and social standing were revamped when, at sixty-two years old, he remarried. In fact, the new bride was his former wife's

> **"Segregation is not humiliating but a benefit."**
> **—Woodrow Wilson**

niece. The two married in a spring wedding at St. Thomas's Episcopal Church in New York City. In no time, Harrison and the Mrs. were back at local parties and concerts, rubbing elbows with the nation's most popular political leaders.

★ ★ ★ ★ ★

EXTREME HOME MAKEOVER

As the presidents have come and gone through its doors, the White House has undergone an impressive array of facelifts and upgrades:

- **George Washington** surveyed the country's new capital and picked out the site for the first president's home during the late

1700s. On October 13, 1792, the cornerstone was laid and construction began.

Buchanan cocked his head to the left because he was nearsighted in one eye and farsighted in the other.

- **Known by a variety of friendly nicknames**, including President's House and Executive Mansion, the first "First Family" home had no name until 1798, when the original sandstone exterior was whitewashed. The facelift prompted the nick name "White House," but the term was initially more popular in England than in America. One hundred years after the residence's construction, Theodore Roosevelt officially proclaimed White House as the mansion's title and the nickname finally stuck.

DID YOU KNOW

Martin Van Buren had large mutton-chop sideburns.

- Although **French Minister Louis Barbe Serurier encouraged him to leave the White House untouched** during the War of 1812 because of its significance as a national landmark, British General Robert Ross burned the building to the ground when his army stormed Washington, D.C. Dolley Payne Madison was able to save a few keepsakes from the fire, however, including a priceless painting of George Washington.

- **As the White House was rebuilt,** President and Mrs. James Monroe sold their personal furniture to the government to permanently outfit the place when he moved in. The charred remains of what used to decorate the interior were used to fill a pit so Monroe could plant a vegetable garden. The remains were found years later by archaeologists when President Ford decided to dig a swimming pool in that very spot.

The teddy bear was named after Theodore Roosevelt. While hunting in the South in 1902, Roosevelt's dogs cornered a bear, but he refused to kill it. His mercy was praised in a newspaper cartoon, and friend Morris Michtom asked Teddy for permission to use his name for the creation of a new toy bear.

DID YOU KNOW

John Adams was not very interested in clothes and was rumored to have worn the same hat for ten years.

Chapter 8

Dead and Gone:
Taken Too Soon

Dead and Gone: Taken Too Soon

On her hit show *Roseanne*, actress Roseanne Barr once said, "If you spend all your time worrying about dying, living isn't going to be much fun." The leaders of America may not have spent much time stressing about when their time would come, but maybe they should have— six escaped assassination attempts and eight died in office. Some barely survived childhood, while others experienced the death of coworkers and family members. From slipping off a log, suffering a serious case of indigestion, or navigating the ridiculous home remedies of their days, they made their deaths (and near deaths) darn inspiring.

> Just as Coolidge entered the presidency in 1924, his son, sixteen-year-old Calvin Jr., got a blister on his toe while playing tennis that caused a fatal blood infection.

★ ★ ★ ★ ★

(ALMOST) SAVED BY THE BELL

The second president to be shot while in office, James A. Garfield might have survived if it weren't for the stupidity of those trying to save his life. Treated for his gunshot wound in the White House for two whole months, Garfield was visited by more than fifteen doctors who wanted to nurse him to health and find the missing bullet lodged somewhere in his body. Probing him with medical instruments and their curious, stubby fingers, the doctors actually worsened the situation by accidentally puncturing the president's liver. Oblivious to their mistake, the group continued their worthless search and called on an old inventor friend—Alexander Graham Bell— to help find the pesky bullet.

After being shot, Ronald Reagan said jokingly, "I forgot to duck."

Bringing his new metal detector to Garfield's room, Bell and his associates scanned the president for any signs of metal in his chest. The thing went haywire, and nobody quite knew why. No one had thought to move Garfield off his bed, which was made of metal springs. When he died on September 19, 1881, an autopsy showed the bullet's true location. Doctors concluded that Garfield could have survived had he simply been left alone.

DID YOU KNOW

Truman escaped assassination on November 1, 1950 when Oscaar Collazo and Griselio Torresola tried to shoot their way into Blair House where Truman and his family were staying while the White House was being renovated. A White House guard was killed, and two others were wounded.

★ ★ ★ ★ ★

SHIVER ME TIMBERS

William Henry Harrison was asking for trouble when he gave the longest inauguration speech in history, outdoors, on one of the coldest days the city had ever seen. In order to appear more prestigious, Harrison refused to wear a jacket and gloves. After an hour and forty-five minutes of shivering through the dissertation-like speech, he fell terribly ill. Although he

DID YOU KNOW

Eight presidents died in office: William Henry Harrison (after having served only one month), Zachary Taylor, Abraham Lincoln, James Garfield, William McKinley, Warren G. Harding, Franklin D. Roosevelt, and John F. Kennedy.

recovered just a few days later, he was back in bed with the chills in no time. Rounds of home remedies—spoonfuls of castor oil, ipecac, opium, brandy, and camphor—were little help and likely worsened his condition. Harrison passed away on April 4, 1841, making him the first president to ever die in office.

★ ★ ★ ★ ★

THE SHOW MUST GO ON

While the length of William Henry Harrison's speech made him the first president to die in office, the length of one of **Teddy Roosevelt's speeches actually saved his life.** As he was preparing to address the crowd at the Hotel Gilpatrick in Milwaukee, Wisconsin, in October 1912, an assassin ran out of the crowd and fired a shot at him. However, the bullet slowed down significantly when it ripped through Roosevelt's thick speech manuscript.

DID YOU KNOW?

Franklin D. Roosevelt contracted polio at thirty-nine. Through rigorous exercise, he learned to stand with braces.

Surprisingly, stubborn Roosevelt insisted on delivering part of his speech with the bullet still in him. Blood soaked the front of his shirt, until he finally collapsed and was rushed to the hospital. The shooter, John Schrank, later said that "any man looking for a third term ought to be shot." Roosevelt later held up the torn, bloody manuscript and said, "You see—it takes more than that to kill a Bull Moose."

An edition of the *Detroit Free Press* described the unlikely event as follows:

> Milwaukee, Wis., October 14—A desperate attempt to kill Col. Theodore Roosevelt tonight failed when a .32-caliber bullet aimed directly at the heart of the former president and fired at short range by the crazed assailant, spent part of its force in a bundle of manuscript containing the address which Col. Roosevelt was to deliver tonight, and wounded the Progressive candidate for President. Col. Roosevelt delivered part of his scheduled address with the bullet in his body, his blood staining his white vest as he spoke to a huge throng at the auditorium. Later, he collapsed, weakened by the wound, and was rushed to Emergency Hospital.

★ ★ ★ ★ ★

You Are What You Eat

After pigging out on cherries and milk at a Fourth of July ceremony at the Washington Monument **in 1850, Zachary Taylor had a bout of severe stomach problems**, got sick from the heat, and—despite efforts to treat him with leeches and opium—died five  days later. Years later, Taylor's body was exhumed because of rumors that his death seemed too unusual to be natural. Was it a result of foul play rather than a terribly embarrassing case of diarrhea? Accusations that Taylor's wife, Peggy, had poisoned him aside, all tests for traces came back negative. Today, most historians say that Taylor likely died of cholera.

★ ★ ★ ★ ★

(Would-be) Independence Day Death

An epileptic and the namesake of Madison, Wisconsin, James Madison was younger than both of his vice presidents—yet both George Clinton and Elbridge Gerry died while he was in office. When it was Madison's time to go, in 1836, White House officials had a brilliant

> It took Garfield eleven weeks to die after being shot by assassin Charles Guiteau on July 2, 1881. He died on September 19, 1881 in Elberon, New Jersey. He was forty-nine years and 304 days old or 10 months.

160

DID YOU KNOW

Two months before his inauguration, the Franklin Pierce family was involved in a train wreck, and their eleven-year-old son, Benjamin, was thrown from the car and crushed to death before their eyes.

idea for how he could ride into the proverbial sunset. They offered him drugs to keep him alive until the Fourth of July so he could pass away on the anniversary of his nation's independence. Not interested in postponing the inevitable for the sake of symbolic romanticism, he refused treatment and died on June 28.

★ ★ ★ ★ ★

 BLASPHEMOUS BIRD

At Andrew Jackson's funeral, in 1845, his pet parrot had to be escorted out of the service for interrupting the solemn event with excessive swearing.

Chester Arthur spent his last years in office knowing he could very well die of Bright's disease before his term ended. He knew that the more active he was, the greater his chance of succumbing to the disease, and yet he even made an attempt to gain his party's nomination for another term.

★ ★ ★ ★ ★

I VANT TO DRAIN YOUR BLOOD

After taking a long stroll to inspect his estate on December 12, 1799—a chilly day of snow, sleet, and rain on Mount Vernon—George Washington came down with a bit of a sore throat. Two days later his condition worsened, and doctors predicted that his lungs and his throat were "shutting down." To try and treat his aches

and pains, Washington's physicians had a bright idea—draining blood out of the former president's body and placing a strip of flannel soaked in ammonium carbonate around his neck.

Not surprisingly, the remedy failed to prolong Washington's life, but it was something other than needles (and the stench of the flannel) that kept him from being able to simply die in peace. He had an intense fear of being buried alive and made his secretary promise multiple times not to put his body in the

DID YOU KNOW?

As a boy, William McKinley nearly drowned in Mosquito Creek in Niles, Ohio.

ground less than three days after his death—just to be sure. (Apparently, Eleanor Roosevelt had a similar fear of being buried alive—she ordered that her veins be cut before her burial.) At sixty-seven years old, Washington died while taking his own pulse. One of the last things he said was, "I die hard, but I am not afraid to go."

★ ★ ★ ★ ★

TECUMSEH'S COY CURSE

Obviously not a fan of the war-mongering white men who continued to steal land from his fellow Native Americans, Shawnee Chief Tecumseh claimed to have placed a curse on William Henry Harrison when he was elected in 1840, proclaiming that Harrison (along with every other president elected in a year that ends with a "0") would be doomed to die in office. Harrison died of pneumonia after just weeks in office. Lincoln (elected in 1860), Garfield (1880), McKinley (1900), Harding (1920), Roosevelt (1940) and Kennedy (1960) also all died before their terms as president were up. The so-called curse was not broken until Reagan was elected to office in 1980, and he was nearly assassinated in 1981.

Reagan's would-be assassin, John Hinkley, wanted to kill the president to impress actress Jodie Foster. After the assassination attempt, he was put in a mental institution.

163

★ ★ ★ ★ ★

SLIPPIN' ON THE DOCK OF THE BAY

As a rowdy young boy, Abraham Lincoln had two close calls with death. At seven years old, he and best friend Austin Gollaher were romping in the woods when Lincoln slipped off a slimy log and fell into Knob Creek. Unfortunately, neither boy could swim. All Gollaher could do to help was hold out a pole for Lincoln to snag. After a few minutes of struggling, Lincoln finally grabbed on and was pulled out of the muddy water. Afraid of what their mothers might say about their dirty clothes, the boys stripped to their skivvies and let their garb bake dry in the sun. On another occasion, at just nine years old, Lincoln was working at a gristmill when he was kicked in the head by an angry mare. Bloody and confused, the boy appeared lifeless until he suddenly awoke shouting the same thing he had said to the mare just before being whacked unconscious: "You old hussy!"

DID YOU KNOW?

Unsuccessful assassination attempts were made on the lives of Andrew Jackson, Theodore Roosevelt, Franklin D. Roosevelt, Harry Truman, Gerald Ford, and Ronald Reagan.

As president, Lincoln had a terrifyingly prophetic dream about his own death before the fall of Richmond during the Civil War. He envisioned that he was in the White House and heard crying from a room down the corridor. When he entered the room and asked who had died, he saw himself in the coffin across the room. Lincoln was assassinated one week later. His killer, John Wilkes Booth, had been plotting the attack for some time. Booth stalked the president from early in his political career and can be seen lingering close to Lincoln in photographs from his Inauguration Day.

★ ★ ★ ★ ★

 KICK THE BUCKET BANDWAGON

During Benjamin Harrison's administration from 1889-1893, a whopping twenty of his friends, family members, and political associates kicked the bucket and left him to his lonesome. Former President Rutherford B. Hayes and Secretary of State James G. Blaine died. (Some physicians reported that the latter simply gave up on life because he "lacked the courage to live.") Harrison's wife also died, and his adorable granddaughter Marthena succumbed to scarlet fever. Despite his grief, Harrison moved on. In 1901, after remarrying and having another child in his early sixties, Harrison died of pneumonia like his grandfather William Henry Harrison, the ninth president of the United States.

★ ★ ★ ★ ★

Last Dance with Ellen Wilson

Famous for his role in ending World War I and overseeing three popular amendments to the Constitution, Woodrow Wilson seemed unstoppable. But just a few months into his term, his beloved wife, Ellen, died and left a depression so deep that he sat stunned by her cold body for two straight days. His sullen demeanor would not heal until after he met and married his

Speaking to reporters about his health, Nixon once claimed that he had never had a headache during his whole life.

166

DID YOU KNOW

Lincoln's son Robert Todd Lincoln was seconds away from possibly being able to save his father's life, as well as the lives of two other assassinated presidents. He had arrived to meet his father at Ford's Theatre just seconds after John Wilkes Booth pulled the trigger. He was on the way to meet President Garfield and arrived just minutes after he was shot as well. Finally, Robert was en route to New York from Buffalo to meet President McKinley the same day he was assassinated at the Pan-American Exposition in 1901. Talk about being at the wrong place at the wrong time.

second wife, Edith Bolling Galt, the following year.

However, by that time, Wilson's health had deteriorated significantly. A stroke in 1906 had left him blind in one eye, and he had high blood pressure and frequent headaches. Another stroke in 1919 left him paralyzed on one side. With that, Edith decided it was her turn to step up to the political plate.

Eventually, she took over many of her husband's responsibilities, serving as a middleman between him and other government officials. She reviewed important documents and made decisions she didn't consider serious enough to bother her husband about. In fact, her leadership earned her the nickname the "Secret President" and the "first woman to run the government."

In 1921, the Wilsons returned to their comfortable Washington home, and in February 1924, the former president's body finally gave out.

★ ★ ★ ★ ★

TOMBSTONE TYPO

As death approached, **Thomas Jefferson wrote his own epitaph**

without mentioning that he served as president of the United States. The tombstone reads:

> There was buried
> Thomas Jefferson
> Author of the Declaration of American Independence
> Of the Statute of Virginia for Religious Freedom
> & Father of the University of Virginia

★ ★ ★ ★ ★

Peachy Keen

Although he did survive the common illnesses that often took the lives of young boys, **Ulysses S. Grant did nearly die twice as a youth**. Once, he fell off a log into a flooded creek. Another time, the unruly horse pulling his carriage nearly dragged him off a steep embankment. Although he survived his own near-tragedies, Grant unfortunately watched one of his friends die when his friend lost control of the horse he was riding and was crushed by the animal.

After leaving the White House in 1877, however, Grant's health began to fail and his financial situation looked even worse. (The Marine Bank had collapsed and left him with nothing. At one point, the Grants had only $180 to their name.) However, a ripe, juicy peach would ultimately predict Grant's painful end. One hot summer day, while taking a bite out of the delicious fruit, he felt a sharp pain in his esophagus. His handwriting suddenly turned from formal to a messy scraggle, and he started to suffer severe choking fits. His cigar smoking had caught up with him, and in June 1885, the general died of throat cancer. The one thing that kept him alive that long, doctors said, was his determined will to finish his book, *Personal Memoirs*.

★ ★ ★ ★ ★

SHOT IN A NEW YORK MINUTE

Excited about a scheduled appearance at the Pan-American Exposition in Buffalo, New York, in 1901, William McKinley could not wait to mingle among the public. Although his personal secretary, George Cortelyou, feared the trip would pose danger, the president disagreed and insisted on attending as scheduled. After crossing the Canadian border to visit Niagara Falls on September 6, McKinley returned to the New York fairgrounds to rub elbows with the common folk.

Although more than twenty-four guards were monitoring McKinley, a young man named Leon Czolgosz stepped forward to shake the president's hand with his bandaged right arm. A .32-caliber revolver was hidden among the bandages. The bullet penetrated McKinley's stomach, and he was rushed to the hospital.

DID YOU KNOW

Some people believe that a casual conversation in a Chicago tailor shop sealed McKinley's fate. There, Czolgosz announced to a friend that he was planning on killing a priest later that year. "Why kill a priest?" his friend inquired. "There are so many priests; they are like flies—a hundred will come to his funeral." Czolgosz must have heeded his friend's suggestion to be more creative and changed his mind, because a few months later he shot William McKinley at the Pan-American Exposition in Buffalo, New York.

Selfless until the end, McKinley worried about everyone else as people ran to his aid. He begged officials not to hurt the gunman and tried to warn his secretary of how his invalid wife might react to the news of his injury. At the hospital, he seemed in high spirits as he shared food and cigars with Pan-American Exposition President John Milburn. Unfortunately, McKinley succumbed to gangrene and died eight days after being shot.

★ ★ ★ ★ ★

THREAT ME BABY ONE MORE TIME

When it came to death threats, Rutherford B. Hayes had more than his fair share. At his inauguration, he was secretly sworn into office because local officials feared a riot would break out and his life would be in danger. Later, Hayes barely dodged a bullet that was fired into a window in his home.

But why was he such a target for assassination? Because he had actually lost the election to Democratic candidate Samuel Tilden. Before the presidential contest began, everyone knew the race would be close. Corruption ran rampant throughout the election—South Carolina, Louisiana, and Florida each submitted two conflicting sets of electoral votes when it came time to count the ballots. Though Tilden won the popular vote, Congress had to set up a special committee to sidestep the three states' screw-up and decide the fate. Unfortunately, eight members of the committee were Republicans and seven were Democrats, so Tilden never had a chance for a fair fight.

WHERE WE GOT THIS STUFF

Beschloss, Michael. *The Presidents*. New York: Ibooks, 2000.

Boller, Paul F. *Presidential Anecdotes*. New York: Oxford University Press, 1996.

Boller, Paul F. *Presidential Wives: An Anecdotal History*. New York: Oxford University Press, 1988.

Caroli, Betty Boyd. "Jacqueline Kennedy." In *American First Ladies*, ed. Lewis L. Gould. New York & London: Garland Publishing, 1996.

Furman, Bess. *White House Profile: A Social History of the White House, Its Occupants and Its Festivities*. Indianapolis: Bobs-Merrill, 1951.

Hunt, Gaillard. *The Life of James Madison*. New York: Russell & Russell, 1968.

Johnson, Paul. <u>A History of the American People</u>. HarperPerennial: New York, 1997.

Lamb, Brian. *Who's Buried in Grant's Tomb? A Tour of Presidential Gravesites*. New York: PublicAffairs, 2000.

Loewen, James W. *Lies Across America*. New York: Touchstone Books, 1999.

———. *Lies My Teacher Told Me*. New York: Touchstone Books, 1999.

Morse, John T. Jr. *John Quincy Adams*. New York & London: Chelsea House, 1980.

O'Brian, Cormac. *Secret Lives of the U.S. Presidents*. Philadelphia: Quirk Books, 2004.

Perret, Geoffrey. *Ulysses S. Grant: Soldier and President*. New York: Random House, 1997.

Pessen, Edward. *The Log Cabin Myth*. New Haven: Yale University Press, 1984.

Phillips, Kevin. *William McKinley*. New York: Times Books, 2003.

Reiger, Kurt and Richard Shenkman. *One-Night Stands with American History*. New York: Perennial Press, 2003.

Roosevelt, James. *My Parents*. Chicago: Playboy Press, 1976.

Sievers, Harry J. *Benjamin Harrison: Hoosier President*. New York: The Bobbs-Merril Company, Inc, 1968.

Winkler, H. Donald. *Lincoln's Ladies*. Nashville: Cumberland House Press, 2004.

WE ALSO USED THESE WEBSITES:

www.allpresidents.org
www.americanpresident.org/history
www.historybuff.com/presidents
www.presidentsusa.net
http://urbanlegends.about.com
www.suite101.com

www.thelincolnmuseum.org
www.civil-liberties.com/factoids
www.apa.org/releases/presidents.html
www.hoover.nara.gov
www.whitehouse.gov/history
www.calvin-coolidge.org
www.archives.gov/exhibit_hall/tokens_and_treasures/tokens_and_treasures
    _home.html
http://archives.cnn.com
www.u-s-history.com
www.acfnewsource.org/art/poli_memorabilia.html
www.pbs.org
http://statelibrary.dcr.state.nc.us/nc/bio/public/johnson.htm
www.apgrolier.com
www.geocities.com/presfacts/bush.html
http://en.wikipedia.org/wiki/Gesture
www.geocities.com/presfacts/clinton.html
http://encarta.msn.com/list_uspresidents/10_Things_You_Didnt_Know_About_U_S
    _Presidents.html
www.cyberbee.com/campaign/music.html
http://www.mackwhite.com/dictator.html
http://www.geocities.com/ultrastupidneal/Knowledge-Fact-President.html
http://www.divasthesite.com/Political_Divas/Trivia/Trivia_Eleanor_Roosevelt.htm

ABOUT THE AUTHOR

Camille Smith Platt is a freelance writer and the Editor of *Chattanooga Christian Family* magazine. A graduate of the Samford University Department of Journalism and Mass Communication, she has also done research and writing for national trivia magazine *mental_floss* and Birmingham lifestyle magazine *PORTICO*. Her love-hate relationship with trivia stems from a fascination of quirky knowledge and a lifetime of always being stumped. She and her husband, Daniel, live in Chattanooga, Tennessee.

YOU MAY ALSO ENJOY THESE OTHER BOOKS IN THE REAL CHEESY SERIES.

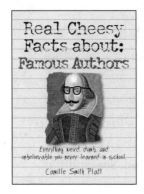

Real Cheesy Facts About: Famous Authors

ISBN-13: 978-1-57587-250-6

ISBN-10: 1-57587-250-1

Real Cheesy Facts About: Rock 'n' Roll

ISBN-13: 978-1-57587-251-3

ISBN-10: 1-57587-251-X

Real Cheesy Facts About: TV & Movies

ISBN-13: 978-1-57587-249-0

ISBN-10: 1-57587-249-8